Praise for *A Cultured Left Foot*

'A superbly nuanced examination of what makes a footballer great'
The Times

'Illuminating interviews provide a raft of anecdotes and tasty sound bites on a fascinating topic ... Quirky and exuberant'
★★★★ Jon Spurling, *FourFourTwo*

'Football may not be about life and death but it's certainly about vision, balance, guts, feet and graft. These are some of the factors considered in probably the most intelligent football book of the year' (No.1, The Ten Best Sports Books of the Year)
Chris Maume, *Independent*

'Okwonga has racked up plenty of air miles and a lot of homework for his essays examining "'the 11 key elements of footballing greatness". [His] determination to find connections in the unlikeliest of places is admirable' *When Saturday Comes*

'[Okwonga] can claim to have produced a rarity: an intelligent football book. His regular references to a multitude of great footballing moments prove he is also extremely well informed, but a guy who can appreciate football's many absurdities ... each of Okwonga's chapters is rich in humour as well as analysis. It is that most enjoyable of reads which can be dipped into on a regular basis' *Yorkshire Evening Post*

'Splendid ... [Okwonga] has put together the season's most enjoyable book about the game, a wonderfully intelligent, football-soaked attempt to define he indefinable. Okwonga is both a renaissance man and a football obsessive, and that's a pretty hard balancing act. He's head over heels in love with the game, yet he remains in touch with the real world and is able to see football's absurdity as well as its passion and beauty ... The difference between very good and great is one that matters – so much so that it sometimes seems to be the whole point of watching sport: to find that point at which a human being reaches his own limits and, with them, the limits of human capability, and then goes beyond. Those who care about this question, those who look beyond mere victory, those who wonder why football holds them in thrall almost despite itself, will have a ball with Okwonga's wild and insightful book'

Simon Barnes, Chief Sports Writer, *The Times*

'Endless fascinating details and anecdotes'

Simon Kuper, author of *Football Against the Enemy*

'A work of insight from a young writer trying to solve an old problem, the definition of that much over-used word in football vocabulary; great'

Martin Tyler, Sky Sports

'Hilarious anecdotes ... a scintillating read, brimming with rich detail ... one book that should find its way onto every football fan's bookshelf. Join the greatness debate'

The Crack, Book of the Month

A Cultured Left Foot

A Cultured Left Foot

Musa Okwonga

Duckworth Overlook
London • New York • Woodstock

This edition 2008
First published in 2007 by
Duckworth Overlook

LONDON
90-93 Cowcross Street
London EC1M 6BF
Tel: 020 7490 7300
Fax: 020 7490 0080
info@duckworth-publishers.co.uk
www.ducknet.co.uk

NEW YORK
141 Wooster Street, New York, NY 10012

WOODSTOCK
One Overlook Drive, Woodstock, NY 12498
www.overlookpress.com
[for individual orders and bulk sales in the United States,
please contact our Woodstock office]

A catalogue record for this book is available
from the British Library

ISBN 978-0-7156-3763-0

Typeset by Ray Davies
Printed and bound in Great Britain by
Creative Print & Design, Blaina, Wales

For my father, my mother, for Miriam, for Wilson, and for my family; for Toni, and for Tom Fenwick, a legend. Finally, for Duncan Mulholland, Richard Eagle and Ollie Broome, three true football men: take care, guys.

Contents

7

Acknowledgements

First I'd like to thank everyone who responded to my questionnaire, and who made this debate so enjoyable.

I'd like to thank especially the following, who gave their time, their guidance and their enthusiasm to make this book possible:

Majid Abdullah; Simon Albert; Giovanni Amedeo; Phil Ball; Robin Balmer; Simon Barnes; Andy Barton; Olivier Bazin; The Beast; Martin Blake; Tom Bromley; Raphael Burke; Papa Chris Bushell; Chopper; Kate Church; John Collins; Vinny Cooper; Caroline and Suzannah at Duckworths; James Edwards; Nick Ferguson; Fuzzy; Lindsay FitzGerald of Axis Podiatry; Matthew Hardwick; Gordon Hill; Lee Hodges; Elly James; Rob Jones; Natalie Kenley; Simon Kuper; Lois and Sean Magee; Neil McCarthy; Hugh McIlvanney; Steven McManaman; Andy Morris; Tyler Nottberg; Alex Payne; James Pryor; Pugs; Maria Ribo-Pares; Matt Ridley; Albert Scardino; Andy Sloan; Squirrel; Patrick Taylor (twice!); Camilla Waite; Vic Wakeling; Paul Walter; Tim Williams; Justin Zaman; Boudewijn Zenden; Pierre Zenden.

Above all, I'd like to thank my agent Heather Holden-Brown, and Nick Webb for showing extraordinary faith in me; and thanks again to my father, who won't get to read this, but who remains as present as my mother in any of the good that I have ever done.

Introduction

What makes a great footballer?

It's the essay to end all essays, it's the football follower's dream assignment; what's that elusive mix of gifts which makes for a Bobby Moore, a Maradona, a Pelé?

There are as many answers to this question as there are football fans, and in what remains the world's sport of choice those responses number a fair few: there's not a stray soft drink can on a street across the globe that hasn't been kicked in homage to the beautiful game. My own view was years in the making: honed through thousands of hours spent watching and weeping as that penalty soared high beyond that crossbar, or reading till knee-deep in needless sporting trivia, or hugging hundreds of strangers in crowded bars because the beauty of that goal, that thirty-yard slalom through that tightest of rearguards or that half-volley so holy it's probably got God shaking his head, has made you embrace each other because there's just no other way you can make someone else feel the perfection of what you've just seen.

So, having my own view, I thought it only right that I should go out and test it against those of other people. I drew up a survey inviting comments on and rankings of the eleven defining qualities that I believed all great players had to possess; eleven wasn't a significant figure, other than being a magical number that everyone associates with football. I sent the survey to everyone I knew, telling them to send it to everyone they knew. And, while their responses rained in from everywhere, be it Malta or Malaysia, I went out and talked to anyone.

Anyone was a late-night conversation with a French friend, discussing the finesse in the finishing of Thierry Henry. Anyone was a series of sports writers, a psychologist, a poet, a broker and a ballet dancer. Anyone was an impromptu judo tutorial with a Holland international, and an hour with the founder of maybe the most successful sporting monopoly in global television. Anyone was a man once revered by Ryan Giggs and now a born-again Christian in Bristol. Anyone was the finest centre-forward the Muslim world has ever seen, and a Missouri father-of-two with the hands of Gordon Banks. Anyone was a courteous Scouser, fond friend of Robbie Fowler and Luis Figo, with an ego tough as tungsten. Anyone was them, and also you.

I learned very quickly that the best way to handle this task wasn't to write it so much as to chair it, as if it were a raucous debate in any given local pub. I walked into several interviews expecting one insight, and walked out with three or four that were entirely different. And I learned, despite over twenty years' immersion in the game, just how little I knew about football. It's true: I knew plenty of football's nuts and bolts, I knew the winners of various trophies and probably even the minutes in which many of the decisive goals were scored; I felt my team's losses so deeply that I couldn't read the sports pages for days afterwards, for fear of being reminded of their defeat. But I wasn't ready for the sheer scope of thought that I came across, and I've included many contributions here.

It was brought home to me more than ever that as a football fan, whether you're Pelé or the village postman, greatness will have moved you, and in infinitely different ways.

Football can make you laugh, love, hate and hurt, and if a footballer's great he can do all of that to you in an instant. A great footballer will need that madness, that blinkered obsession, which blinds him to any outcome other than victory. But he'll also need to see everything; he'll need vision of boundless sweep, to play the pass or strike the drive that'll draw glory to him. He'll have to summon as much grit as grace from the depths of his boots, and while he must play as hard as he can, he has to remember to have fun; to remember that, after all, he's only playing.

In this book, I aim to show you a range of things: why the game's leading figures thought Gascoigne was greater than Lineker, why Brazil's Ronaldo was great not once but twice, and why a dog had more fun playing the game than Roy Keane. But most of all, with this long and broad look at those who've illuminated football's past and present, I aim to show you what its rising stars will require to light up its future. I have written it partly as a semi-serious analysis, but mostly as a statement of my infatuation with football, which I still don't fully understand and therefore know will never end. And, since I've been given this chance to put together a study of those who were the best at the thing that I love the most, it'll always be the best piece of homework that anybody ever gave me.

MO, May 2007

Feet

If you support a football team, then your choice of football team isn't really a choice at all: it's as much a choice as your skin colour or the hand that you write with. In each fan's life there's a seminal moment that binds him or her to a particular club for life, which makes them realise that they're truly hooked. It could be that time that they go for a kickabout in the park, and – for some reason even they don't understand – they find themselves impersonating a certain player. Or it could be the time that they're listening to the final scores on Saturday on the BBC, and when they hear that Grimsby or Hartlepool or Luton Town have lost, tears escape their eyes. But what it really comes down to in many cases, and definitely in my case, was falling in love with feet.

To admit to falling in love with feet is something that raises eyebrows and arouses scorn at the best of times, so a swift explanation's needed. Before I knew of Manchester United's romantic past and its richer-than-thou present, I watched Norman Whiteside in the 1985 FA Cup final against Everton. The game was goalless, and moving deeper and deeper into extra time, as the nineteen-year-old Irishman skipped inside off the right wing and curled a delicate finish past Neville Southall to win the match. Where did you get feet like that? I tried to copy Whiteside's strike a thousand times in my back garden, standing behind the washing line and pretending that its damp sheets were a defensive wall around which I could bend the ball. The grass in that patch of garden was worn as barren underfoot as any cornfield harassed by locusts, and the apple trees – which I was naturally using as goalposts – had their branches broken so often with stray shots that one of them almost stopped growing fruit altogether, perhaps out of protest at their treatment. But, despite all that damage to my garden's ecosystem, I never did a Whiteside.

But there's one thing that I did share with Norman Whiteside, and that was a distinct lack of acceleration. A common argument is that if you're slow, then there's no chance that you'll make a great player, which was a claim levelled at Whiteside. I disagreed: the game was replete with stars not notable for their pace, such as Argentina's Juan Román Riquelme. They made up for that lack of pace, I felt, with 'fast feet': the skill of switching the ball from foot to foot with the deftness of a croupier shuffling cards. This view of mine was to meet with fairly strong opposition, but more of that later.

At my primary school – Marish Middle School, near Slough – most of the boys and several of the girls were similarly obsessed with feet. The feet most coveted were those of Liverpool's John Barnes, and dozens of us tried to recreate his moves each morning before the first bell for lessons; studies, at that point, were the painful but necessary punctuation of our journeys into this obsession. Later, at prep school in Sunningdale, I would wildly envy the feet of my teammates Ollie Broome and Kaunda Kavindele, both of whom could do wonderful things with both their right and left.

Broome, whose older brother Giles held the record for goals scored in a single school season – thirty-six, in just over twenty matches – was quickly making a name of his own. Lean as a carrot, with a copse of curled brown hair, Broome possessed feet that were likely to be found making a fuss on the edge of the opposition box, his cheeks permanently red in sympathy at their efforts. Broome was soon able to do what Norman Whiteside once did, curving the ball around or over vainly leaping opponents; Kavindele, whose father Enoch was once the vice-president of Zambia, sauntered about the pitch in a fashion that was appropriately statesmanlike. He was perhaps the more gifted of the pair; though one of the youngest members of our team, he already played with the casual irreverence of a boy in his mid-teens. He was short, sudden and compact, a smile never far from his face, that grin fitting the mischievous corners of his mouth like a good suit. Every footballer has grown up alongside feet like those of Kavindele, and they're all the more humble for it; his feet whirred about the ball as if they were forming crop circles, so joyfully busy that at the end of each match his own boots

14

wanted to put their feet up. Years later still, when I was languishing in Eton College's second and third teams and Broome was the creative fulcrum of the first eleven (or, as it was a little pompously called, The Association), I would want his feet even more. The ball obeyed them as if summoned by a three-line whip. But I never really wanted my own feet, and that's because they were too big.

There's that old and persistent saying that all of the best footballers have small feet, and as I grew older I found more and more examples within Manchester United's very own ranks to support this harsh and apparent truth. Ryan Giggs was a size seven, Wayne Rooney, a size eight-and-a-half; even Rio Ferdinand, tall and broad as he was, was only a size eleven. I was a size twelve, with feet flat as the soles of flippers, so there was little hope for me on that score. Vainly, I looked for examples that would give me hope. Nwankwo Kanu, the fitfully brilliant Nigerian who won national and European titles at Ajax and Arsenal, was rumoured to have enormous feet; the BBC, reporting on the 2000 African Cup of Nations, confidently asserted that he had 'giant size-15 boots'. However, in a preview for the 2002 World Cup, *Sports Illustrated* said that they were in fact size fourteens, whilst in the same year Barry Glendenning wrote in a *Guardian* match report of 'Kanu who shuffles his size 11s'. Given, if anything, that feet are supposed to grow with the passage of time, something was amiss here.

In my search to find a link between foot size and footballing ability, I came across the findings of WPST, a radio station in Princeton, New Jersey. WPST had breezily compiled a list of attributes that people with unusual feet were supposed to have, a list which had me peering anxiously at my own odd pair. I was 'among the thinkers of the world', I noted smugly, because I had long toes. My feet were wide, which meant that I was a hard worker with strong family values; however, they were not webbed, which indicated that I was not the life and soul of the party and would not make a good salesperson or entertainer. Most intriguingly, the radio station revealed that if my second toe was bigger than the others, then I was dependable, conservative and could keep my emotions in check. I held my feet up to the light in turn and considered them. The second toe of my right foot actually seemed to be longer than the second toe of my left foot – I hadn't noticed that before, it's funny what you pick up on when you look closely enough – but, on both feet, they seemed about the same length as my big toe. I wasn't sure whether that made me conservative or not. WPST didn't say anything about football, though, and in any event they didn't seem to know how big Kanu's feet were.

To find that elusive connection between great footballers and foot size, I stayed on Norman Whiteside's trail. Having retired early through injury, he had gone to study podiatry at the University of Salford. It was here that I contacted Lindsay Fitzgerald, a musculoskeletal podiatrist; Fitzgerald had worked with the England women's football team at the 2005 European championships, and so, if anyone should be able to resolve this issue, it was her. Do great footballers have to have small feet?

'No!' she laughed, a little incredulous. 'No, that's not something I've come across. I suppose you choose the sport you're built for. People who are big generally go into rugby, people who are smaller generally go into football.' Having chalked this down as an urban myth, we moved into more serious territory. The investigation made by her five-year PhD, a course that she was just over halfway through, was whether there was a relationship between an athlete's core stability – that is to say, their balance – and the workings of the foot. This research was the first of its type; given the amount of money in football, and the fact that such knowledge could perhaps prolong a player's career, I was surprised that this area hadn't been covered before. But, as Fitzgerald pointed out, much of the thinking about an athlete's centre of gravity had simply been assumed. She'd found that, when examining problems with footballers' feet, she had to consider the body as a whole, with seemingly remote areas such as the spine all playing a part in the injuries that she saw. By extension, then, it was logical that other unexpected areas of the body, other distant muscle groups, might be affected by the misadventures of the foot.

Talking to Fitzgerald, I realised that, as far as physiology went, football was the biggest misadventure that the foot had ever got itself into. Players' boots, she observed (almost in despair, like a dentist forced to perform intricate surgery on the same patient yet again), were too often worn 'too tight-fitting ... they're not designed for the natural anatomy of the foot, they're like ladies who walk round in narrow heels all the time'. What's more, when running, according to *Sporty Feet* (a paper that she'd co-authored), 'an average-sized man will process 112 tons of weight through each limb per mile': it's easy, then, to see why so many footballers end up with osteoarthritis, the classic wear-and-tear injury, after their careers have ended.

Of course, the game's best players have flown in the face of such dangers, and have learned to express themselves with every part of their feet. Ronaldo, in the 2002 World Cup semi-final against Turkey, scored the winning goal with a toe-poke: one of the most technically advanced footballers of his generation, he used the same part of his foot that all beginners do when they're trying to hit a ball with maximum power. Ronaldo had become so good that he took the game back to basics, making it as simple as if played by a child.

Simplicity is often seen as the hallmark of genius: Paul Dirac, a winner of the Nobel Prize for Physics, commented that he could tell if his equations were correct because they looked beautiful. And just as the deceptive simplicity of Albert Einstein's most famous equation, $E = mc^2$, masks the brilliance that conceived it, so some of the greatest goals consist of one easy motion, the long swing of a foot. Marco van Basten's volley against Russia in Munich, in the final of the 1988 European Championships, is arguably the best example of such thinly-veiled magnificence. As a cross was launched forward from a position deep on the left wing, the Dutchman made a looping jog in towards the far post, six yards beyond the shoulder of the ball-watching defender. At the precise moment when the dropping ball came to him, dipping suddenly behind the Russian rearguard, van Basten was standing square of the goal, too distant to pose either an instant or a serious goalscoring threat. And then van Basten, perfectly balanced like the best of equations, swung his right foot, his leg a slow, elegant pendulum: his boot caught the ball as it was ending one flight, and sent it on a new one, a high and stately arc into the top left-hand corner of the net.

Feet such as van Basten's are rare: feet that can cushion and cannon-fire the ball in the same motion, that in the same breath are both soft and severe. Of course, van Basten's feet failed him at the tragically young age of twenty-seven, an injury to his Achilles tendon forcing him from the game in the mid-1990s. However, so many had fallen in love with his feet during his years at Ajax and AC Milan that his retirement gave rise to one of the most beautiful scenes anyone could wish to see in their own honour. In Milan's San Siro stadium, that vast, steep-sided amphitheatre which holds eighty thousand fans, he walked alone down the centre of the pitch as a full house stood and rained down seemingly eternal applause. Meanwhile, Fabio Capello, the coach whose obduracy was the stuff of legend, wept openly.

I'd always thought that, if a player could dribble as well as had the Dutchman, then a lack of speed wouldn't be a bar to his greatness. Paul Scholes has never been the fastest player, but his sharpness and swiftness of touch have always created sufficient room for him to work, even in the busiest of centre-circles. I put this view to Hugh McIlvanney of *The Sunday Times*, who was wholly unconvinced. We'd met for a coffee during a typically busy London lunchtime: talking with him about the beautiful game was a little like having a tutorial with the Professor of Football at Oxford University, if they'd had the wisdom to create such a post there. In one hand he clutched the sheaf of papers, marked with a series of notes and corrections, that comprised the two sample chapters that I'd sent him, and in the other he brandished what he called a 'stogie', a long, wheezing cigar that carefully trod a carbon footprint across the air of the Strand. With the public-place smoking ban now in force, we'd sat outside the coffee shop so that we could allow the stogie to breathe. McIlvanney was one of those few journalists who'd become a presence in his own right; America's Jim Murray, as vivid a chronicler of Muhammad Ali's work as McIlvanney had been, was another. It's rare to be almost as much a part of football's fabric as one of the players; the scribes are looking on enviously from the outside. Yet he'd been acquainted with George Best down the years – though not closely, he hastened to add – as well as Sir Alex Ferguson, and had been granted almost exclusive access to the Brazil camp during the 1970 World Cup. For now, though, he was disagreeing with me about speed.

'Pace has always been very valuable', he told me, feeling that by leaving it out of my eleven elements I had made a 'blatant omission'. 'It is such a huge consideration', he'd continued, 'genuine quickness has always been a devastating quality, and those without it really stand out. For example, Kenny Dalglish is one of the great players without pace, he's one of the great slow players – slow being a comparative term, of course.' McIlvanney felt that great players were mostly quick, and that those like Dalglish were merely the exceptions that proved the rule.

Yet Dalglish was such a glaring exception that he almost served to defeat McIlvanney's point. Here, after all, was a man who'd won six league titles and three European Cups at Liverpool, and who'd also been placed first in a vote by over one-hundred-thousand of that club's fans for 'The 100 Players Who Shook the Kop'. As Ronnie Moran said of him: 'He wasn't the quickest of movers, but he was twenty yards quick up here', said Moran, placing his finger on his temple, 'and he'd be in position before the defenders knew what was happening.' And what feet; though his left was his weapon of choice, he was unafraid to strike free kicks with his right, the mark of a truly two-footed player. Nor was his right foot merely an item of brute force, the driver that he'd draw out when the sand-wedge wouldn't do; it brought Liverpool the European Cup in 1978, with a calmly-clipped finish against FC Bruges to give them a 1–0 win. That was typical Dalglish: in the penalty area, he stabbed endless loose balls away from defenders and into his stride in the same sweeping motion. This was a region where, to coin the American phrase, he had 'the guts of a burglar'.

Dalglish's furtive and deliberate manner on the pitch was matched by his self-possession during interviews, a trait which had once moved McIlvanney to remark in an article that the day Kenny Dalglish became a gusher of controversial quotes, stones would be queuing up to give blood transfusions. Indeed, Dalglish outdid himself when speaking to the journalists for that aforementioned 'Shook the Kop' compilation. After a procession of club greats from Liverpool's past and present, including

Ron Yeats, Jamie Carragher and Steven Gerrard, had flitted across the screen to declare their adoration of him, Dalglish was called upon for comment on his first place in this poll, and on the fact that Gerrard had finished in second place. 'I thought he'd have beaten me, Steven', said Dalglish, not quite managing to contain a knowing smile. Gerrard's an exceptional player, and is swiftly developing a legend of his own, but Dalglish was so good that he deserves to be placed at once among the handful of the best ever European footballers: alongside, if not above, Michel Platini.

But, Dalglish or no Dalglish, McIlvanney wouldn't be denied. 'The lack of pace has very plainly been a limiting factor in the career of Beckham', he pointed out. 'The absence of two major attributes – pace, and the capacity to go beyond opponents with trickery – have been very serious in Beckham's case. Although I have the highest regard for the qualities that he does, or at least did possess – for example, he was probably one of the best kickers of a ball in the world for a while, and as a delivery man from wide positions, he did very well – when people talk about him as a really great player, then they're dealing in exaggeration.'

David Beckham's feet: so famous that when he broke a bone in his left foot before the 2002 World Cup, everyone suddenly knew exactly where the metatarsal was, and even the Queen was moved to ask about its wellbeing. But how great were Beckham's feet, specifically, his right one? McIlvanney saw him as one of the best kickers in the world: if we look back over the decades, it's hard to remember anyone who's struck the ball more cleanly over such remarkable distances. Beckham's free kicks have been revered for some time, but his long passing is almost peerless. Ruud Gullit and Glenn Hoddle were his closest competitors in this field, but even they couldn't comfortably send sixty- or seventy-yard cross-field passes with no loss of accuracy. Xabi Alonso has emerged most recently as a challenger in that area, and he and Beckham are among the few players whose mere distribution of the ball would make for an engrossing highlight film.

But Beckham's failure to adapt to a much-coveted position in central midfield, given his stellar success on the right wing, reveals his play as one-dimensional. The centre demands not only a quick mind, which Beckham has, but equal speed in the feet, and too often Beckham would be caught in possession whilst trying to turn away from trouble. The room that you have on the wing when you're aiming to pass your opposite man, that vital space, no more than a couple of feet, either side of him into which you can manoeuvre, simply doesn't exist when you make your way further infield. The irony is that Ryan Giggs, Beckham's former running-mate, has made the transition to this playmaking role with relative ease; it's worth asking whether, were Beckham's feet more versatile, he might have had more of a future at Old Trafford. The departures of both Beckham and Ruud van Nistelrooy from Manchester United were trumpeted as the result of personality clashes with Sir Alex Ferguson, but Roy Keane was indulged far longer than the pair of them and with far worse behaviour. The sales of both players to Real Madrid can be regarded primarily as footballing decisions: van Nistelrooy, though a goalscorer without parallel, lacked the lithe instincts of a forward who would be just as happy running the channels as through the middle, and so the focus of Manchester United's attack became too narrow, too predictable.

So a great player – or at least one that Sir Alex Ferguson is willing to hang on to, which given some of his transfer market travails might not amount to the same thing – is one whose feet present several troublesome options to the opposition. I maintained that pace wasn't a necessary option among those, but looking at the career of Brazil's Ronaldo, it was initially hard to argue with McIlvanney's point. There was profound sadness in Italy when Ronaldo, then at Inter Milan, suffered severe damage to his knees in the late 1990s. At that point, he had already been twice elected as the FIFA World Player of the Year, in 1996 and 1997. Bobby Robson, in his foreword to James Mosley's *Ronaldo: The Journey of a Genius*, is emphatic that 'if he managed to stay free of serious injury, he had every chance of becoming the best footballer ever. And I stand by that.' Ronaldo went on to play a starring role in the 2002 World Cup, scoring eight times in seven games as Brazil took the trophy in Japan, but was in the eyes of many – to coin proudly that old cliché – just not the same after injury. For a striker like Ronaldo, what's so cruel about a partial loss of acceleration is that it brings a certain dullness to other areas of your play. In *The Heart of the Game*, Jimmy Greaves wrote that Gary Lineker possessed 'that sudden burst over two or three yards which distinguishes the great from the good … what elevates good to great is that first yard, which is in the head.'

It may be heresy to suggest that Ronaldo was slightly, but tellingly, less aware in the latter part of his career, considering that his return from injury included that aforementioned World Cup triumph and a transfer to Real Madrid, where he was the league's top scorer as Real won the 2003 La Liga title. But some would say that the Ronaldo of 2003 was merely brilliant, and that the Ronaldo of 1997, who scored 47 goals in all competitions for Barcelona in a single season, was simply matchless.

His feet were that good. After one game against Atletico Madrid, whom Barcelona had pulverised 5–2 at the Nou Camp, his opposite man – relieved, doubtless, to have heard the final whistle – said that he felt as if he had just been marking four players. In an age where football salaries have ascended into orbit, or at least towards the realms of those who work at hedge funds, Ronaldo can be said to have made defenders sweat for their afternoon's pay cheques. He was, even more than Pelé had been before him, a danger from anywhere in the enemy half of the pitch, capable of beating several men either with the dribble or with what has been called 'the sprint within a sprint', a phrase used to describe the moment where an athlete, seemingly already at full speed, squeezes an extra surge of pace from his calves and moves clear of the chasing pack. And then there was the stepover, always that same combination of right foot rolled over the ball then moving away on the left, and always that same result, a trail of flapping limbs and broken souls left in his wake. Whether he was scoring a hat-trick of individual goals against Valencia, or charging through six challenges to score one of the goals of the century at Compostela, he approached goal with the inevitability that's the hallmark of every great athlete.

Some fans, like Sir Bobby Robson, might lament the lost years of Ronaldo's career and his subsequent, subdued return, wondering what might have been. But it's better to see this period as inspiring. Knowing that he'd lose some of his famed speed off the mark, Ronaldo learned to make different movements in and around the box, relying instead on the sharpness of his one-touch football and evolving from a panther to a poacher. This is the type of progression of which Michael Owen has taken note: whilst the play of the Brazilian and the Englishman has seemingly become more prosaic with the passing years, it's also arguably much more efficient. Ronaldo also deserves special praise for being one of the few footballers in history to have become great twice: once with pace, and once without it. The first time that he became great, in that 1997 season, his speed with the ball at his feet was his prime asset. The second time that he became great, in 2002, his feet were less frantic, but uniquely decisive, relying now on short sidesteps to create room for his startling shooting from distance.

Arsenal's Arsène Wenger, whose thinking is as advanced as that of any manager in world football, seems to have identified speed as of equal importance to technique in all of the players that he buys. His selection of young talent, as multicultural as any crowd you'd find milling in Heathrow's Terminal Four, all have that in common; from the Englishman Theo Walcott to Emmanuel Eboué of Côte d'Ivoire, each of them move with an urgency that threatens to render obsolete the flat-footed centre-back. In an era of increasing defensive sophistication, Wenger's philosophy is that speed is the key which will spring the trap. Even the players traditionally regarded as more static in terms of their positioning on the field, such as Kolo Touré or Brazil's Denilson, are surprisingly spring-heeled. Given Wenger's record of three Premiership titles in ten years, and a narrow loss in the final of the 2005 UEFA Champions League, we can expect his next Arsenal team to be perhaps the most dynamic and dangerous factor in Continental football in the decade ahead. (Once, of course, that is, they learn how to finish.)

One of Ronaldo's compatriots, and a man whose gifts would've been perfectly suited to Wenger's playing style, was arguably the quickest off the mark of all. Romário da Souza Faria, or Romário, took his own special brand of football to leading clubs in both Europe and South

America, including PSV, Barcelona and Vasco da Gama. That brand consisted of an unmatched arrogance, and acceleration that might have shamed an Olympic track star. No slouch himself, Ryan Giggs has commented that 'he was just lightning over three yards, it really was unbelievable to watch. Romarío would do a Cruyff turn and before you knew it, he'd be gone. He'd leave players for dead and whip the ball into the back of the net.' For most of the match, Romarío would shuffle about the pitch, almost as somnolent as a possum, convincing defenders (and, on occasion, possibly even himself) that he was utterly disinterested in proceedings. It was only then, once they'd discounted him as an imminent threat, that he'd make a flat, sharp sprint across the face of the back four, cradling the through-ball in his stride and coursing on towards goal.

Romarío understood better than anyone that effective football's all about fooling your opponents into accepting the tempo at which you're playing, and then switching it at a split-second's notice. That's how he plotted one of the goals in his legendary hat-trick against Real Madrid in the 1993–94 season. During that 5–0 victory in the Nou Camp, he took the ball on the edge of the box, softly cupped it in his right instep, swivelled past the last man – and, as Giggs would've warned – he was away. The manner of his finish was also of note, a stab with the outside of his boot into the bottom corner. Romarío seldom scored with powerful shots; like the Tottenham Hotspur and England predator Jimmy Greaves, he preferred to roll the ball into the net, as if reluctant to part with it or do harm to it.

Yet these weren't merely compassionate feet, they were also lazy ones; Romarío's other famed reluctance related to training. So great were his innate gifts and the ego that accompanied them that he often refused to practise, a trait he shared with AC Milan's Dejan Savićević, dubbed *Il Genio* (The Genius) by his club's owner, the adoring Silvio Berlusconi. As Patrick Vieira testified in his autobiography, 'He was the one with the most talent but actually he trained very rarely. For a Sunday game, he'd only really show up from the Friday onwards. I never saw him do a full week's training ... because he was amazingly talented, though, [the coach] Capello let him do his own thing.'

Vieira saw a connection between talent and hard work, namely, that the more you had of the former, the more you did of the latter, but that rule didn't apply to The Genius. It's often remarked that players who rely so much upon their natural technique are more inconsistent than most; the reason typically given is that it's difficult to produce brilliance as a matter of routine week in, week out. That may well be, but it can't help that they are indulged as readily as was Savićević. Nevertheless, in Milan's case he proved excellent value for money. Signed from Red Star Belgrade, where he'd played a decisive part in their 1991 European Cup final triumph over Olympique Marseilles, he proved to be even more instrumental in the same tournament in 1994, as Milan crushed Barcelona in the final in Athens. Of Milan's four goals without reply, he scored the brilliant third, a swirling lob from the right flank that drifted over the stranded Zubizarreta.

Savićević struck that shot with his left foot, a part of the body that has almost mythical qualities. Maradona, the greatest left-footer of them all, has illustrated this point with a story about Roberto Rivellino, one of the stars of the 1970 Brazil team:

> [Rivellino] was in Brazil's *concentración* in Mexico '70. Doing nothing, because those guys didn't need to do anything to play. And so there he was, sitting around with Gerson and Tostao ... Then Pelé shows up. And they thought: *This fucker, what can we say to him? He does everything right, the son of a bitch*. So Rivelinho [sic], who always had an answer for everything, thought of what to say. He looked Pelé straight in the eyes, he was already the best in the world, and said: 'Tell me the truth, you would have liked to be left-footed, right?'

Sadly, Pelé's response to this jibe wasn't recorded. But Rivellino knew that, as a left-footed player himself, he'd be readily associated with a particular elegance, with a romantic style of play to which Pelé was not privy. Certainly, there's a long and illustrious list of great left-sided sportsmen – Hungary's Ferenc Puskás, Portugal's Paulo Futre – who have graced football, and left-handers like John McEnroe who have graced tennis. And in even asking whether the left-sided player is particularly blessed, the sporting world is something of a beacon of enlightenment; for centuries, left-handers in Europe have suffered scorn, suspicion and persecution, as has been noted by Dr Nick Neave of the University of Northumbria. 'The word "left" in English', writes Neave, 'stems from the Anglo-Saxon *lyft* meaning broken or weak and this tendency appears to be universal as the French word for left – *gauche* – also means clumsy or crooked; Italian is *mancino* derived from the word *mancus* meaning crooked or dishonest; and the Latin word for left is "sinister", derived from *sinistrum* meaning evil. In Russia, to be called a *levja* (left-hander) is an insult.'

But on the football pitch, the left-footer – although he is, as the Angles and Saxons would have it, 'broken-footed' – has a natural advantage, as do his cousins in other sports. As Porac and Coren found in *Lateral Preferences and Human Behavior* (1981), 26% of baseball pitchers were left-handed, a percentage which rose to 48% among the top fencers. Given that the overwhelming majority of players – around 80% – are right-footed, the left-footer benefits from the fact that he's a challenge which opposing defenders will rarely face. What's more, as he attacks goal, he'll be dribbling on his stronger foot towards the defender's weaker foot. When a left-footed player adds to that fact the gifts of stunning acceleration and close control – as did, for example, Bulgaria's Hristo Stoichkov – then the package is irresistible. It also seems to explain why left-footed players are often so wholly dependent on that foot, why it will be said that a player such as Chelsea's Ashley Cole is 'all left foot'; with such an advantage, why would a left-footed footballer concede it by regularly using his right?

But whether left-footers are touched by genius is a different matter. It needs a closer look, which was taken by Carey et al. of the Department of Psychology at the University of Aberdeen. Their comprehensive report, *Footedness in world soccer: an analysis of France '98*, was published in the Journal of Sports Sciences in 2001; it looked at the pattern of foot use by a sample of 236 players from 16 teams at the 1998 World Cup, and was proudly announced as the first of its time. The researchers saw several instances where players, whether their right or left was their dominant foot, would shy away from using their other foot. As they write, 'Players can be seen going to great lengths to try and position the ball for a shot with the preferred foot, in spite of a clear opportunity for use of the non-preferred foot.' Amongst the most skilful players, such as Paolo di Canio, these great lengths might go as far as the stylish *rabona* – translated literally from the vivid Spanish as 'cow's whip' – which involves striking the ball by swinging your kicking foot behind your standing leg. In Maradona's case, the *rabona* was an effective technique for crossing the ball; in di Canio's case, which really sums up his career, it appeared in his repertoire as a party trick.

Carey et al. go on to mention two examples of the 'strategic consequence of being a rare left-sider'. One of those, the lack of opponents' familiarity, has been discussed above, but the other is the 'additional possibility ... that the left foot of a left-sided athlete has "privileged access" to the visuospatial networks of the right cerebral hemisphere'. To put this in crude and reductive layman's terms, the left foot is 'cleverer' or more 'cultured' than the right foot; or there's Ray Clemence's timeless assessment of the left foot of Gheorghe Hagi, which was so good that it 'could open a tin of beans'.

Sadly, Clemence didn't explain why a foot's ability to open a tin of beans was a litmus test for genius; but, in any case, the suggestion that the left foot operates on a higher plane of intelligence seems to have been conclusively rebutted by the research. Carey et al. found that 'remarkably, both left- and right-footed players were as skilled, on average, with their non-preferred foot as they were with their preferred foot, on the rare occasions when they used it. Therefore, it is unlikely that infrequent use of one foot compared to the other foot can be accounted for by skill differences between the feet.'

So the genetic supremacy of the left-footer is a fiction, although that won't stop romantics such as Rivellino from believing it. There are also several such romantics in England, who've largely attributed England's failure to win a major international tournament since 1966 to the fact that its national team lacks left-footed players of world-class stature – as opposed, of course, to lacking a sufficient number of players of world-class stature coached by a manager of world-class stature. John May, of BBC Sport Online, went so far as to refer to this situation as a 'left-side crisis'. The argument runs that without a right-footed right-winger and a left-footed left-winger, opposing teams won't be stretched sufficiently wide in defence; they'll keep the play in the congested areas of midfield, stifle England's football, and make it difficult for them to score. But the irony is that the England team that won the 1966 World Cup was famous for its lack of width, to the extent that it was nicknamed 'the wingless wonders'.

What's more, some of the most successful left-wingers of modern times have been right-footed, such as Arsenal's Robert Pirès. The Frenchman scored 62 times in 189 matches for the London club, an exceptional ratio of goals-to-games for someone who was essentially a playmaker. It may be, then, that the left-footed question is a red herring. The wider issue for England should be to develop more players who are equally adept at using both feet, and it seems that this area is a matter of both coaching and confidence. As Carey et al. conclude, 'The most interesting result to emerge from this study is the magnitude of foot preference (80–85%), in spite of the considerable skill apparent in the non-preferred foot.'

But the real concern in English football isn't whether the game's being played with the left foot, the right foot or both; it's in the failure of successive generations of training staff to produce genuinely penetrative dribblers, men whose sudden shuffles can whisper 'Open Sesame' to the most stubborn of defences. The Premiership is the home of the most rapid football on the planet, but there are too few Englishmen who have the art, at the game's very highest level, of beguiling a defender from a standing position with a succession of feints or step-overs. Encouragingly, those who can are from a younger generation – Wayne Rooney, Aaron Lennon – but the pickings are still relatively slim when we look at teams such as Portugal, where players such as Ricardo Quaresma, Nani and Cristiano Ronaldo have already honed this art so early in their careers.

There have also been rumblings of discontent amongst football's older order that football in general is becoming more physical and less technical. Incidentally, these doubts have been expressed by two famous left-footers: by Saudi Arabia's Majid Abdullah when I spoke with him, and by Romania's Gheorghe Hagi in a *World Soccer* interview in 2001. 'Today', Hagi said, 'you seem to be considered good only if you can run fast, or are physically strong. What about individual skills?' It wasn't as if Hagi would have had much to lose from this establishment of a new, more athletic order: not only did he have superb technique, he was also broad of frame with a fearsome fifth gear. But artistry was his true calling card. Whenever a player emerges in a vaguely similar form to a previous great, there's a rush to see him as a young pretender, rather than a star in his own right. And so Robinho of Real Madrid and Brazil is the new Pelé; Wayne Rooney was the new Gascoigne; and Pablo Aimar, the frail and mercurial Argentine forward, was unfairly tagged the new Maradona. But least deserving of this treatment was Hagi, who was patronisingly christened the 'Maradona of the Carpathians'. Whereas Robinho, Rooney and Aimar were all young players who might have expected this treatment, Hagi was an original who'd earned the right to his own legend, and not to be a mere branch of someone else's.

Like all the greats, Hagi's only limits on the pitch were those that he chose to impose upon himself; his feet seemed truly to come alive only in major tournaments, and he spent largely ineffectual periods at both Real Madrid and Barcelona before finally flourishing at Galatasaray, with whom he won the UEFA Cup in 2000. But what was marvellous about Hagi, despite his inconsistency, was that although he was so much more gifted than his colleagues he had no hesitation in playing for the team. And vain feet are too often the downfall of a potentially great player.

Simon Kuper, the celebrated sports journalist and author, gave me one of the more recent examples of this: Juan Sebastian Verón, who spent two frustrating seasons at Manchester United following a move from

Lazio in 2001. 'He lost interest in football', said Kuper, 'and he kept giving these pretty passes … Zidane, for example, almost never gives a pretty pass for the sake of it. He always gives a really functional ten-, twenty-, thirty-metre pass, exactly into the guy's feet, so he can do something with it. Now Verón would sort of lean back and he'd hit a fifty-metre pass into somebody's chest, who'd two defenders on him. And it's a great pass, but it's indulgent … he's a bit of a showman.' This was a scathing assessment of a man who'd cost Manchester United a transfer fee of £28.1million, then (briefly) a British record. Verón won a championship in his vastly-improved second year, but his time at Old Trafford is generally regarded as a failure, given his team's lack of success in the UEFA Champions League during his stay.

I didn't know that this was entirely fair; I'd found Verón's feet more stubborn than selfish when he was at United. He'd been ceaselessly spectacular in Serie A, and so when things didn't go so well at Old Trafford he'd resorted to extravagant trickery to inspire himself out of his slump in form, whilst he should have played short, sharp passes to regain his confidence. This failure of his feet to change gear from the sublime to the simple was much of what did for him.

Whilst Kuper spoke of Zidane's precision in possession, Phil Ball, in *White Storm*, concentrated on his economy. 'He spends an alarmingly short time with the ball for a player of such repute', remarked Ball, 'and yet it is precisely this quality that lends him his greatness'. Zidane knew that this was the most disruptive way to play, that by staying in possession for a good while he'd allow defenders some continuity, some comfortable rhythm into which they could settle. So he chose to be brief, keeping the opposition on edge as to when he might decide to influence the game, a leading actor waiting hungrily in the wings.

In the same work, Ball also suggested that there was such a thing as too much speed. 'Exceptionally fast players rarely become greats', he wrote, 'a truth well illustrated by the present European incumbent of the "quickest" label, Barcelona's Dutch import, Marc Overmars. Dangerous player though he can be, his speed seems to have an inverse relationship to his effectiveness, for he rarely, if ever, seems to cross the ball successfully to his teammates.' Ball had been a little harsh here on the now-retired Overmars; the reason why Overmars' crossing was not world-class was the same reason why Thierry Henry rarely scored headed goals, which was that both players were so often leading the line of counter-attacks that sending over a high cross, or receiving one, was seldom a skill that they were given the chance to practise.

When quick feet are mentioned, the Brazilians are the first footballers to come to most people's minds, followed by the Dutch and the Eastern Europeans. Germans aren't generally regarded as being amongst the world's finest dribblers; their game's condemned as dour and functional. Even their greatest players haven't escaped this stigma. Lothar Matthäus, whom Maradona rated as the toughest opponent he had ever faced, was an attacking midfielder of grace and guile for Bayern Munich and Inter Milan. However, he was invariably described as aggressive and powerful. Elsewhere, the craft in German football has often been downplayed, to the extent that there are few football fans who would say that they have any affection for German feet.

The irony, then, is that AC Milan's Kaká has been so roundly praised ever since he first arrived before an adoring audience in the San Siro, because Kaká, although a Brazilian, has German feet. His dribbling is generally free from the elaborate step-overs that are expected from South Americans, and he plays with a simple, classical style, taking two or three touches on average whenever in possession. Steven Gerrard knew this painfully well, having witnessed Kaká's 45-minute symphony in the first half of the 2005 UEFA Champions League final. Gerrard, remembering the Brazilian's hand in Milan's seizure of a 3–0 lead by the interval, has said, 'Kaká was a great player, I knew that. Anyone who starts for Brazil must be special. But not until I spent that half, running around after him, chasing his shadow, did I appreciate how quick he was in possession. Never in my career had I encountered anyone as fast with the ball at their feet. Kaká was lightning.'

Bournonville, a Dane who in the nineteenth century crafted a series of light-hearted and well-loved ballets, wrote in his *Choreographic Creed* that 'the high point of artistic skill is to conceal mechanics and effort under a harmonious calm', and on that basis he'd have welcomed Kaká's efficiency of touch. The art in Kaká's play isn't to be found so much in what he's doing with the ball, as in the lack of fuss with which he's doing it. In a similar vein, in the *Ballet Companion*, Eliza Gaynor Minden wrote that 'Bournonville technique exemplifies modest grace without apparent effort ... it has a dancy quality that never compromises the integrity of lithe, seamless phrases for the sake of a single step.' A dancy quality: that's the style with which Bayer Leverkusen played on their way to two major finals in the 2001–2 season, yet it's hard to escape the feeling that they'd have received more lasting appreciation if they were a Dutch or Spanish team. Michael Ballack was the crux of that Leverkusen team, a German who would have been welcomed as a holding midfielder in the Brazilian team, but whose skills have largely been met with respect as opposed to adulation.

And the best feet, it seems, literally do have a mind of their own. In 2002, engineers at the University of Sheffield's Sports Engineering Research Group, Yamagata University's Sports Science Laboratory and Fluent Benelux conducted research into free kicks by, among others, Michael Ballack and David Beckham. Fluent Benelux, a company that is 'the world's largest provider of computational fluid dynamics (CFD) software and consulting services', creates software 'for simulation, visualization, and prediction of fluid flow, heat and mass transfer, and chemical reactions'. Its Director of Marketing Communications, Dr Keith Hanna, was astounded by their findings. He said that 'it still amazes me that elite soccer players like Beckham and Carlos do what they do in a free kick instantaneously and under immense pressure in critical games. Their brains must be computing some very detailed trajectory calculations in a few seconds purely from instinct and practice. Our computers take a few hours to do the same thing and although we can now better explain the science of what they do, it is still magical to watch.'

Roberto Rivellino, for his part, has summed up succinctly how he was able to bend the ball such that even David Beckham would have been mildly envious. As he explained to *The Guardian*, 'To start with, you've got to be able to really whack the ball ... It goes left, then swings back to the right – hopefully swooping and dipping so the goalkeeper doesn't know where it's going. Often the striker of the ball doesn't even know!'

So the best feet have intelligence, whether it's conscious or otherwise; in Rivellino's case, it seems to have been a particularly glorious case of hit-and-hope. The best feet also have their own trademark: for whilst there are many footballers who can produce the same given piece of skill, it's only the best feet that can claim to own it. Were you to watch footage of certain footballers – the greatest ones – where everything had been blacked out save their feet, you could instantly identify who they were. Zidane had his pirouette, a double-drag-back during which, for the briefest moment, he seemed to stand proudly atop the ball like Nelson upon his column. Ronaldinho has his 'flip-flap', a sudden snap of his right foot that threatens to throw his own ankle loose from its socket. And, of course, Johann Cruyff had his turn, that elegant swivel where the ball's scooped behind the player's back with his instep, and beyond the lunging defender.

Cruyff's play was also notable for its deceptive plainness. 'I never practice tricks', he once said, 'I play very simply. That's what it's all about. Playing simple football is the hardest thing … Simple play is also the most beautiful. How often do you see a pass of more than 40 metres when 20 metres is enough?' Zidane's feet didn't only have simplicity; they also had that crucial quality known as 'end product'. As Simon Barnes, the Chief Sports Writer at *The Times,* has written, 'Many of Zidane's moves would have looked flash if performed by anyone else. But they were never performed for themselves, always in the context of the search for victory. Zidane was a player with an immense sense of style, but style was always remorselessly subjugated to content. He never played the virtuoso for the sake of it, it was a temptation he was immune to.'

We talk often of feet with narrative, feet that always seem ready to tell a compelling story, but that's not how we describe it; we say instead that an expectant hush falls whenever the ball reaches a certain player's feet. And that hush, when it descends, signals the arrival of a future legend like nothing else. In his autobiography, Steven Gerrard talks of a similar silence when Wayne Rooney first set himself apart: when 'one day, in training at Slaley Hall, Rooney announced to the whole England squad the massive size of his talent. We were playing a practice match towards the end of training when Rooney picked up the ball, dribbled past a few players and chipped Jamo [David James]. Astonishing. Silence reigned for a split-second, as if everyone was trying to take in exactly what we had just seen. Then we all burst into applause, everyone, even established stars like Becks and Owen. We all glanced at each other to say, "This boy can play". Only seventeen, and already heading for greatness.'

When Zidane was discovered, his control was so dextrous that it was said that he had feet where his hands should be; when Rooney was discovered, the same could be said of him. That's the lasting irony of the greatest players and their feet: thousands of years since they evolved from apes, they've developed so far that they can again use their feet as if they were their hands.

Balance

Balance: not so celebrated a gift as quick feet, but an equally vital attribute of any great player. After all, it's that freakish ability to remain upright despite the two-pronged lunge of a defender's late tackle, to duck and bob happily as a buoy on the ocean's waves. Those who have it often seem to have a lofty, disdainful demeanour on the field; which is why it's a quality that's been typified in recent years by that most aloof of midfielders, Michael Ballack. Balanced men such as Ballack seem to enjoy the discomfort they cause in those who try, and fail, to fell them. The proud pivot of world-class midfields at Bayer Leverkusen, Bayern Munich and Chelsea, as well as the captain of his country, he's imposingly tall, with a steady and square stance; given the casual manner with which he addresses the ball, you could imagine him waltzing in the face of a hurricane.

Which is effectively what he did whilst at Leverkusen, when faced by Liverpool in the UEFA Champions League: he was confronted by Steven Gerrard, at that point the coming hurricane in British football. However, Gerrard spent most of that match on the wrong end of a powerful storm, allowing the German to surge past him and conjure two decisive and very different goals. One was a magnificent header, bearing his twin hallmarks of a sly sprint into the area and an explosive contact with the airborne ball. The other goal he owed all to balance. Thirty yards out, drifting ever central, the ball at his feet and his entire weight rocking towards the right, he sensed Gerrard careering towards him. Then, as the Scouser arrived, Ballack glided left with an easy roll of his shoulders, leaving Liverpool's talisman to slide on by to tackle nothing but turf and the cool spring breeze. All that remained was for Ballack to advance a couple of yards and with minimal warning – the slightest lift of an arm to signal the shot – thrash a left-footed drive above and beyond the dive of Jerzy Dudek. In *The Ballet Companion*, Eliza Gaynor Minden wrote that 'you can always spot ballet dancers no matter where they trained. They're the ones with regal posture, beautiful muscles, and turned-out legs. Even walking down the street most dancers can't help it: they stand lifted and tall.' It's a description that could've easily applied to Ballack.

To find out more about this German's sturdiness, I spoke with Maria Ribo-Pares, who'd been working at the English National Ballet for almost eight years and who was now a first artist. The connection between ballet and football had long since ceased to be a fanciful analogy; several teams were using Pilates exercises as part of their training routines, the more enlightened coaches having seen past the perceived effeminacy of the art form to its various and tangible benefits. According to Ribo-Pares, Ballack's size in this context was neither help nor hindrance.

'I think that it's not a matter of height, it's a matter of proportion. There are a lot of ballet dancers who are very tall', she said. '[With balance] the trick is all in the stomach – if you've got control of those muscles, you're in control of the rest of your body. It all comes from there. From the moment you start dancing, you have to pull your stomach in', explained Ribo-Pares; 'you have to "squeeze your glutes", so that your body is as flat as an ironing board, like someone's punched you. Your ribcage has to be really flat, so that it feels as if you almost can't breathe. So though dancers look very brittle, they have to be very strong.' So that's how Ballack had achieved what the football writer Phil Ball had described to me as his 'don't-fuck-me strut', I thought. It was nice to know that he'd had to struggle at least a little for his indifference.

Ballack's apparent heir at Chelsea, John Obi Mikel, comes from a similar physical mould, and the Nigerian already appears set for a memorable career. Towards the end of the 2006–7 season, Mikel occupied the base of the midfield diamond, a position formerly claimed by none other than Claude Makalélé. No light responsibility, this, as it effectively meant that his manager José Mourinho was handing him the keys to the team's tactical safe. A defensive midfielder has to be more sure-footed than most; in a closely-fought match, he stands in the only lane that a pass can take out of a crowded centre-circle, so he needs to be able to step smartly off either foot at a moment's notice to intercept that ball. That's Mikel's forte, and one which should see him, in the next three to four years, becoming one of the very best players in his position.

Mikel and Ballack are two of only a few big men blessed with balance; normally, it's the preserve of the more diminutive members of the footballing clan, of rapid wingers such as the Dutchman Marc Overmars or Ireland's Damien Duff. The most eminent of them all, however, was the man widely regarded as Glasgow Celtic's greatest ever player, Jimmy Johnstone. The qualities of 'Jinky', as he's fondly remembered, have been captured most memorably by Hugh McIlvanney, who's remarked that 'at times, watching him change direction in mid-stride, you felt he must have a crotch of cast iron ... His exceptional balance enabled him to rock and sway and tumble through tackles like an acrobat and, though he buzzed and flitted as elusively as an insect, he had the sturdiness of a pit pony.'

Though Jinky probably didn't litter German idioms about his speech, *Schadenfreude* seemed to be a guiding principle for him on the pitch. As McIlvanney has somewhat gleefully noted, 'The wee man ... operated on the principle that the surest way to destroy defences was first to demoralise them.' But that wasn't the only principle that Johnstone had operated on; there were other, more impressive forces at play. I'd known before speaking to Lindsay Fitzgerald that good balance was based upon a low centre of gravity; what emerged from my conversation with her was that good balance, in fact, had another element. This was *proprioception*, a word that I found difficult to pronounce at first, constantly putting the prio- before the pro-: it refers to the messages that the joints transmit to the brain, or, as the neurologist Oliver Sacks has described it, 'That continuous but unconscious sensory flow from the movable parts of our body (muscles, tendons, joints), by which their position and tone and motion is continually monitored and adjusted, but in a way which is hidden from us because it is automatic and unconscious.' Lindsay Fitzgerald called this sense 'an awareness of the space around you', a summary which suggests that balance is really just another aspect of the gift, to be discussed later, that is vision.

In that same book by Sacks, *The Man Who Mistook His Wife for a Hat* – an excellent book with which to pose on the train, by the way – he provides a case study for what he has considered a hidden sense, almost, in the words of C.S. Sherrington, 'our secret sense, our sixth sense'. Sacks tells the story of Christina, a young woman who literally overnight lost her sense of proprioception; that's to say, that she was unable to move her limbs without watching them. He writes thus of her predicament that 'standing was impossible – unless she looked down at her feet. She could hold nothing in her hands, and they "wandered" – unless she kept an eye on them. When she reached out for something, or tried to feed herself, her hands would miss, or overshoot wildly, as if some essential control or coordination was gone.'

Christina's condition was thankfully rare, and one to which she adjusted with surprising speed. Jimmy Johnstone, on the other hand, was at the opposite end of this scale; supremely aware of his feet, he rarely had to supervise them as they ran with the ball between them. This ability, to dribble with his head up, was an almost unfair asset. It virtually gave him a bird's-eye view of the game, allowing him those vital split seconds to glimpse space beyond defenders whilst they floundered around his ankles.

So, with his *Schadenfreude* and his proprioception, Johnstone had two mildly tongue-twisting reasons for his balance. Garrincha had both of these; he also had polio, which caused his famously awkward gait. It's commonly considered that Garrincha developed into a great player despite this childhood ailment, but Lindsay Fitzgerald suggested that it might actually have been the key to his success. 'The fact that he had those biomechanics means that his stance was probably quite wide', she said, which would result in good core stability; 'but somewhere up the kinetic chain, it must have affected him later, either through back pain or pain in his ankles.' Due to his alcoholism, Garrincha's kinetic chain didn't have a chance to play a significant part in his demise; which is just as well, since it would've been a quirk of fate too far to have been brought low by the same deficiency that once raised him to the heights.

Another South American, Argentina's Lionel Messi, is on his way to Garrincha's heights, and it's his balance that will take him most of the way there. In the 2007 semi-final of the *Copa del Rey*, the Spanish equivalent of the FA Cup, the Barcelona forward scored a stunning individual goal against Getafe that was hailed as equal to Maradona's second strike against England in the 1986 World Cup. Whilst some quibbled over the fact that Maradona's goal was greater, since it had been netted in a match of far greater importance, there was no disputing the technical quality of what Messi had done. In one respect, he'd achieved parity with 'El Diego': travelling along a line of movement eerily similar to that of Maradona's earlier masterpiece, he had carved a path through the heart of the Getafe back four, before rounding the goalkeeper and clipping the ball home. What Messi and Maradona shared, above all, on their identical journeys through these defences was the simplicity in their dribbling. In fact, they'd hardly dribbled at all, in the conventional sense of using trickery: they'd both simply scuttled forward at tremendous speed, in an almost coldly functional fashion. When a player has perfect balance, he can do that; he's blessed with a change of direction so sudden that the merest sleight of his shoulder is enough to set a defender rocking on his own heels. This ability unites the game's greatest dribblers, from Messi to Maradona, to two of Britain's finest, George Best and Ryan Giggs.

When Giggs reached national prominence at the age of seventeen, making the left flank of any ground that he graced a thoroughly unpleasant place for defenders to spend a Saturday afternoon, he was endlessly compared to George Best. Giggs was very much the junior partner in this comparison, and long after Giggs retires – even though he has won many more trophies and awards than Best ever did – he will in many minds remain so. However, of the pair of them, Giggs arguably owns the bragging rights to the finest goal: a demonstration of balance under pressure that's as statuesque as any ever witnessed.

This strike, in the 1999 FA Cup semi-final, passed instantly into legend, a sixty-yard run past or through six Arsenal players that ended with the ball being thrashed past David Seaman at his near post. It decided the tie 2–1 in favour of Manchester United, who would go on to defeat Newcastle at Wembley. Giggs' unwitting accomplice in this masterpiece was Arsenal's Patrick Vieira, who'd played the ball perfectly to his feet some fifteen yards within the Manchester United half. Viewed again and again, it's increasingly unclear who Vieira's intended recipient could have been other than Giggs, since there were no other players from either team near that patch of turf at the time.

But Giggs felt no sympathy for this slip. Seizing at pace on Vieira's misplaced pass, he surged forward, the line of his run thrillingly direct, a straight sprint towards the heart of the Arsenal rearguard with the ball giddily riding the laces of his left boot. Vieira approached to redeem himself, but fell away like a leaf in a gale; Giggs weaved between three similarly windswept defenders, twice fizzing past Lee Dixon, before evading Adams at the top of the box and hammering the ball high into the net. As the commentators discussed this goal after the match, there was a sense that the Arsenal defence, at that point statistically the most frugal in Europe, had capitulated before Giggs. It was remarked that Giggs had barely altered the angle of his charge, and the ball, apart from one mesmerising moment when he'd switched feet on the edge of the area, had barely deviated from its course. Most of the panel therefore wanted to know why Arsenal hadn't managed to make a challenge. Only John Barnes, who'd visited many similar ills on opponents in his own playing days, knew better. 'His balance is very good', he said simply.

Wingers of the ilk of John Barnes played as if it was a badge of honour to remain on their feet, even though opponents were often hurtling in to hurt them: it's a code of conduct a little like that of the hardened boxer, who'll return to the fray each round despite the promise of more punishment. It's an irony, then, that wingers such as Holland's Arjen Robben, despite having all the balance that a footballer could wish for, seem so prone to falling over when defenders wander near them. These unsightly tumbles to earth, which have latterly stained the sublime résumés of Didier Drogba and Cristiano Ronaldo, mark an age-old cynicism in the game which has attracted growing scrutiny. Whilst we've always acknowledged the existence of the professional foul, it's probably time to make room in our sporting vocabulary for 'the professional fall'.

Practitioners of the professional fall might privately see it as a high form of dark art. Whilst many fans might not like it, there's a certain gymnastic aptitude needed to deceive a referee into thinking that you've been tripped when, in fact, the only thing that's made contact with you is the evening air. If we're being pragmatic, it's easy to see the value of being a good diver, seeing how often penalties and free kicks will decide close contests. It was comforting, then, to speak with Liverpool's Boudewijn Zenden, who, like Barnes, seemed to relish the honest confrontation that I'd always seen as the winger's role.

I caught the train to Liverpool to interview Zenden, and made my way from the station by bus to Melwood training ground. As I moved through West Derby Village, it struck me how residential was this setting. Liverpool, in so far as a multimillion-pound enterprise can be, was a team of its people. The club's facilities sat squarely within the densest of suburbs, flanked by long, seamless streets whose homes sat politely, if a little uncomfortably, shoulder to shoulder. From the outside, Melwood looked like a half-hearted boot-camp; its walls were high, but not insurmountably so, and slits had been carefully chipped into them at various points, so that you could peer easily at the action within.

There wasn't any action that day. With a league fixture against Chelsea only a handful of days away, most of the first team were resting, and only the injured players were required. Zenden, recovering from an operation on his cruciate ligament, was one of them. Harry Kewell, I noted from the visitors' book, was another, the winger having been endlessly failed by his physiology since he'd arrived at Anfield. At Leeds United, this mercurial Australian had been too briefly viewed as one of the finest attackers in the world, scoring seemingly at will in important European matches against Italian defences little known for their charity. I'd arrived fifteen minutes early for the interview, and so I'd the chance to sample the emptiness of the training centre, and therefore to empathise with Kewell as he went through his daily hell.

Hell: I use that word advisedly. The French writer Jean-Paul Sartre wrote that 'hell is other people' (*l'enfer, c'est les autres*); but that can't have been right in Kewell's case. I suspected that, in his current predicament, hell was having nobody else around. Melwood was easy to imagine on a busy Thursday morning: players either racing about the pitch or rolling about it with laughter, the soft turf kissing each pass as it rolled crisply overhead, and then you had Melwood now, Kewell's Melwood, vast and empty as the outback. It was almost easy to imagine the rustle of tumbleweed across the foyer.

Kewell might have wondered what he'd done to deserve his lot. As recounted in *A Season On The Brink*, Guillem Balague's elegant account of Liverpool's 2005 Champions League triumph, Liverpool's coaching staff 'had realised that [Kewell] was a quality player but that he had too many physical complaints and lacked concentration in training and matches'. But even if Kewell's apathy had contributed to a longer period than he should have spent on the treatment table, to have to endure this lonely workplace was a harsh punishment. Ireland's Paul McGrath, a legendary centre-back for his country, Aston Villa and Manchester United, described that experience in his autobiography. 'Over time', explained McGrath, 'injury becomes a state of mind for the sidelined footballer. The first thing you lose is the capacity to be hopeful. The rituals of rehabilitation just wear you down. You pine for the open spaces of training, the banter, the aggression even, when all you see – day after unending day – is the medical room, the table. You are like a cartoon character that has been erased from the page. Rubbed out. Deleted.'

Zenden, by contrast, was far from invisible, and seemed to have got much of his bounce back: he raced up and down the stairs to fetch some coffee, looking like he'd shaken off the last of his serious ailments. I asked him, amongst other things, about balance; he was suitably qualified to discuss this area, having had a useful career in judo before committing himself fully to football. It turned out that this martial art, which, above all others, preached how you should roll with the punches, had informed much of what you could call his gladiatorial approach to playing on the wing.

'Judo is like football', he said. 'It's one-v-one, and there's no place to hide once you step onto the *tatami*. I mean, where are you going to go? There's only one way you're going to get past, and that's to beat this guy.' Eager to further this analogy, he stood up to illustrate his point. 'If you have to throw somebody, you have to work with your own balance, plus with the other guy's balance. Judo is not an aggressive sport, it's defensive, and to be self-protective you have to learn to use the opposition's power to throw him.' He motioned towards me with his hands. 'Let's say, if you pushed me, then I would use your power to roll you over.'

He was only making a demonstration, and not actually asking for me to kick off with him, which was just as well; a former district champion, he'd been awarded a First Dan black belt at the age of fourteen, the earliest possible age at which he could have reached that level. Although he was probably somewhat ring-rusty, I considered it best not to risk my chances.

Zenden's take on the game seemed to be a refreshingly old-school one, pleasing to those of previous generations who feel that football's no longer truly a contact sport. When discussing the merits of past and present players, fans too often concentrate on the current era, forgetting or understating the magnificence of what went before: that's one reason why I went to speak with Vic Wakeling, who could be relied upon to provide the broadest possible perspective. As Head of Football, then Head of Sport, then Managing Director of Sky Sports, Wakeling had played a major role in the extraordinary flow of money into the top level of the game over the last fifteen years. In 1992, Sky had obtained the live and exclusive rights to cover Premiership football, in a deal worth £305 million over five years. This monopoly, only recently ended by the Premier League's grant of rights to Setanta, had taken Sky to the headiest of commercial heights, entrenching it as a global player in the worlds of media and sport.

Wakeling therefore had a vast influence on football; in 2003, Henry Winter of the *Telegraph* thought him the third most powerful figure in the game, behind only Gordon Taylor, Chief Executive of the Professional Footballers' Assocation, and Richard Scudamore, Chief Executive of the Premier League. However, despite the prominence of his work, his public profile was almost negligible, as I found when I began my background research for his interview. I barely had a lead to go on by way of character profile. First, there was *The Times*' mention of the 'enormous loyalty' that tennis commentator Mark Petchey felt towards Wakeling; second, there was a description of him by snooker promoter and Leyton Orient chairman Barry Hearn as 'unique'. Hearn was a friend of Wakeling's, so the sentiment expressed was a warm one, but that didn't make it any less mysterious. So it was, feeling both intrigued and greatly underprepared, that I headed across London to his office.

An indication of Sky's wealth came as soon as I stepped out of Osterley tube station, perched somewhat morosely on a blustery outcrop of West London. There was a shuttle bus that ferried people to and from the Sky campus, with a frequency – every twenty minutes – greater than that of London Transport's apathetic service. The Sky complex, when I arrived there, was vast and vaguely militaristic; it was a sort of Pentagon of popular entertainment, with a series of checkpoints, barriers and speed bumps. Deep in the guts of this fortress, in the seventh of its nine buildings, I found Vic Wakeling.

Having known almost nothing about Wakeling, I was building an impression of him virtually from scratch, so I spent the first couple of minutes of the appointed hour making a mental portrait of him. The first thing that I saw was the small forest of cigarette butts in the ashtray on his desk, several upturned stubs amid a mossy bed of ash. Then there was him; about five-ten, his hair veering ever towards grey, and his gaze – through large though unshowy spectacles – friendly, but of a schoolmasterly intensity. He accompanied this with an accent that was a clipped brogue, and had a great certainty in his speech, which he punctuated regularly with the words 'of course', and would say 'isn't it' in a tone that made this phrase sound not like a question but an invitation to agree.

Wakeling had grown up in the North East, and was a Geordie. He also seemed to be of that important breed, a 'football man'; that's to say, he'd spent his whole life in the game, leaving college and going to work in newspapers as both an on-the-road and desk reporter in the North East, the Midlands and London for twenty-five years, before moving into television. Now in his late-fifties, he'd been working at Sky Sports for almost sixteen years; and so, as he put it, 'I've watched a lot of football over the years.' With that in mind, I asked him about the best player that he'd seen; he gave me his answer, but preceded it with a lengthy caveat: 'All of the player polls that they carry out now and then, of course, are false; because if you had a poll for Manchester United's best player, well, there aren't enough people alive who saw George Best, so all the young fans, of course, are going to vote for [Eric] Cantona. Give them a couple of years, and Cantona will no doubt slip to second or third place, because they'll all vote for [Cristiano] Ronaldo. So all these polls are a waste of time, and they don't prove anything.'

Having said that, he still had his personal favourite. 'George Best … Without doubt, the best I've seen. And, if you speak to everyone around at the same age, from the same era, most of them will tell you exactly the same thing. If we'd had then the number of cameras and the kind of technology that we have now, that we put on the likes of Thierry Henry and Cristiano Ronaldo, [Best's skill] would look twice as good now as it did then. You'd have loved to have had our technology, our cameras, with the way that we can now get tight on their feet … you'd love to have shown that skill to the world. The world is aware, because even with the technology as it was, he looks outstanding. But, I promise you, we could have made him look ten times better.'

That was difficult to imagine. Decades later, George Best remains the epitome of balance on a football field: there can't be many players who took so much pride in being impossible to fell. There's an astonishing piece of highlight film where Best is scythed by a tackle to his mid-section, the force of which assault would have toppled many larger men: Best sways towards the floor, springs back up with the aid of his outstretched fingertips, and sweeps back towards goal, barely impeded by the sprawling midfielder. As Sir Alex Ferguson has noted, 'Here at Old Trafford, they reckon Bestie had double-jointed ankles. That it was a physical thing, an extreme flexibility there … he could do those 180-degree turns without going through a half-circle, simply by swivelling on his ankles. As well as devastating defenders, that helped him to avoid injuries because he was never really stationary for opponents to hurt him. He was always riding or spinning away from things.' On the most famous occasion, against Chelsea in the FA Cup, Best is counter-attacking. He's moving towards goal, unaccompanied by teammates whom he's long since left in his slipstream, when from his right arrives Ron 'Chopper' Harris with a tackle even more late than it is illegal, a dozen studs tearing towards his legs with the blur of an angry chainsaw. But Best absorbs the contact so easily that it's as if his ankles are made of air, rounding the goalkeeper to score one of the goals of that or any other season: it's hard to see how Sky could have made this footage look any more remarkable than it already does.

Wakeling also recalled the time when Best had arguably shone his brightest: it was 7 February 1970, when Manchester United met Northampton Town at the County Ground in the fourth round of the FA Cup. 'If you look back at the state of the pitch that day, it was awful', said Wakeling, 'and he was skipping across mud-heaps.' (As for the game's outcome, Manchester United won 8–2, and Best scored no fewer than six.)

When we're talking of greatness in football, we must remember how important is its aesthetic quality, much of which is rooted in balance. Balance makes a footballer look right. George Best's name is routinely put alongside those of Maradona and Pelé, even though he achieved significantly less at club and country level than either of them; the reason for this must be that he was the purest of footballers, just as they were. To watch Best run with the ball was to see a perfect demonstration of that art. That's why young players like Messi cause such expectation in us: because in even their shortest sprints they remind us instinctively of how the great players should look, and thus make us all the more excited as to what they might grow into.

Fun

'There must be some kind of way out of here, said the joker to the thief.'
So roared Jimi Hendrix at the outset of *All Along the Watchtower*, four of
the most exhilarating minutes of music ever recorded. With this line, the
joker and the thief begin to plot their escape from a corrupt and decadent
kingdom, whilst both a wildcat and an angry wind wail in the background. With this line, Hendrix could also have been describing a
conversation between Dwight Yorke and Andy Cole, as they stood
within the straitjacket of a belligerent Barcelona defence. They were in
the Nou Camp with Manchester United for a group game in the 1999
UEFA Champions League. Yorke – ever the joker, with a smile as
dazzling as the distant floodlights – and Cole, the penalty box pick-
pocket, were forty-five yards from goal, and the angles were all wrong:
the Spaniards' centre-backs were beautifully positioned, blocking the
path for any potential pass. Except, that is, until Yorke and Cole decided
to have fun.

From the right flank Roy Keane clipped a brisk, square pass infield to
Yorke, who tore towards it as if it were the last bus home, but as it
reached Yorke he stepped across it, allowing it to roll into Cole's path;
Cole, dropping a shoulder, instantly released the ball to Yorke, who'd
raced on ahead; Yorke, two yards and two split seconds later, having
drawn two defenders, slid the ball back to Cole, a ricochet of passes that
had set his partner free on goal and Cole, calmly picking out the bottom
left-hand corner of the net, guided the ball there with a firm side-foot.
(By this point, the ball itself was probably grateful for a rest.)

This goal was an inspired piece of havoc, of which Jimi Hendrix's
troublemakers would have been proud. Frank Rijkaard, on his website,
delighted in the simplicity of a sequence of one-twos, whilst taking
pleasure in its playfulness. 'As a kid', enthused Rijkaard, 'playing football

in the neighbourhood with my friends, one of the first satisfactions of the game I experienced was the one-two combination. It was about this feeling and understanding between two teammates that resulted in out-playing one or even more opponents. In fact, it is one of the most simple and effective ways to leave the enemy looking like they have no right at all to be on the game'. And as Yorke and Cole showed, there's much to be gained from taking a joyful approach to sport when great prizes are at stake.

One-and-a-half-thousand years before their double-act in the Nou Camp, the Greek historian Plutarch told the story of the Gordian knot. Alexander, a young soldier from Macedonia, had found his way to the town of Gordium. Here, as Plutarch wrote, there was a 'famous chariot fastened with cords made of the rind of the cornel-tree, which whoso-ever should untie, the inhabitants had a tradition, that for him was reserved the empire of the world'. All that Alexander had to do was untie the chariot, and, so the prophesy went, he'd conquer the earth. As with so many of these ancient trials, it was easier said than done: several brave and brilliant warriors had been defeated by this challenge, this knot that was tied impossibly tight. But Alexander was made of more resourceful stuff. Seeing that the chariot was attached to the knot by a pole, he simply pulled the pin out of the top of the pole, and the chariot fell away from the knot. Alexander, fresh from this triumph, went on to take the whole of Asia, and became known as Alexander the Great. The 'Gordian knot', meanwhile, passed into legend as a seemingly impossible situation that could be resolved with a single stroke.

Rabah Madjer was faced by a Gordian knot of his own, on one May evening in 1987; it was the European Cup final, and the Algerian forward was playing for Porto against Bayern Munich. Bayern, who'd won this trophy on three previous occasions, were only thirteen minutes away from a fourth triumph, leading as they were by a deftly-angled header from Ludwig Kögl. It was then that Jean Marie-Pfaff, the Bayern goalkeeper, palmed a skidding shot to the feet of Madjer, who was standing four yards out with his back to goal. Were he to turn and shoot, the German defender, who was scrambling across the line, would have had a good chance of smothering the ball or hacking it clear. But Madjer, fearless, thought of what would be the most fun thing to do: he back-heeled the ball softly into the furthest corner of the goal. Just three minutes later, he flighted in a cross from the left, which was converted by Juary to give Porto their first ever European Cup.

It's only a special footballer who, confronted in the heat of a match with mounting pressure and mounting odds, will look at all of the available options and select the one that he finds most amusing. The option to look out for at a moment like this is the chip, a method of scoring so rarely practised that it's almost an endangered species. The chip looks as easy as all of the most difficult skills in football: it's the hallmark of the game's cheekiest players, and therefore its best. It's employed to greatest effect when the game's pace is somewhere between frenzied and frantic, the ball skimming across the greasy turf and finally finding itself at the feet of the striker at the area's edge; and he needs to move quickly, because the key to success in football is to change the gear of play so suddenly that your opponent is transfixed, and it's in this breathless moment that the striker, eighteen yards from goal and sixteen yards from a goalkeeper who's wandered too far from the safety of his line, releases the chip. With thuggish intent he jabs his foot at the base of the moving ball, leaving his studs rooted in the earth as the ball rises swiftly and sharply forward; and as it approaches goal it loses speed, fizzing with backspin, so that by the time it reaches goal it's slowed to a gentle loop; but the goalkeeper, beaten by its flight, is long since power-less.

Kaunda Kavindele loved the chip. I saw him do it, in the most ridiculous match that I'm ever likely to be a part of. Cothill House had come to Ascot to play Sunningdale. They'd travelled all the way from the small village of Cothill in rural Oxfordshire, a two-hour pilgrimage by minibus to our home ground, which was a shrine to football. The grass was trimmed like the fast outfield of a cricket square, and the autumn breeze ran itself gently across it, like an uncle's affectionate fingers ruffling his nephew's hair. Under the September sun, the turf took on a softly golden sheen, and the crisp white touchlines framed the pitch like the proud edges of a portrait.

When the two teams kicked off, then, we were obliged to produce something that was artful. Farce is what we made instead. Two minutes from the end of the thirty-minute first-half, our spectators had witnessed seven goals, three of them in our favour: with the incessant to and fro of the football, they must have had necks more sore than if they'd been watching tennis from half-court. As usual, Broome had been imperious, but it didn't help Cothill that their entire back four had apparently been stopping to admire his work, waving this insurgent through to goal like corrupt Customs officials. We didn't dare to look at the face of our coach Nick Dawson, who was our referee that day; he watched helplessly as our team also abandoned all attempts at defence, and he was biting the end of his whistle so hard in repressed fury that I thought he might digest it. Kavindele seemed blissfully oblivious to Dawson's rage – he always did. It wasn't that he didn't care; it's only that he never seemed to do anything wrong, and in that moment when he chipped it, he brought order to those thirty minutes of chaos.

From Broome, he received a square pass, which skipped across to him at an impatient pace, slightly frustrated as the player who'd released it. Twenty yards from goal, drawing his left foot back as if ready to kick a door down, he then swung it gently forward, maybe summoning the spirit of Van Basten. The ball, grateful for this soft slice instead of the battering it had expected, being treated kindly for the first time in the whole of that first half, looped into the top left-hand corner of the goal as leisurely as a grain of pollen on a lazy wind. All eyes then turned back from the ball towards Kavindele, who in this most frenetic of matches had just done the slowest and therefore the most beautiful thing of all. He was still standing in the spot where he had struck the ball, and he was howling with laughter.

Nick Dawson, relieved to have reached half-time at four goals apiece, even managed a smile during his team-talk – he'd caught the good mood from Kavindele – and then sternly told us that we'd go out there and win the match. We didn't need asking twice, and we did so, by eight goals to four. Kavindele, having inspired us, rose to heights even greater than those of Broome, and indeed matched him for genius throughout the rest of the season. But, sadly, I never saw him chip again.

There are other, no less illustrious friends of the chip, such as Ronaldinho, as David Seaman saw in the 2002 World Cup. There was also Didi, a World Cup winner in 1958 and 1962, who pioneered the art of the *folha seca* (the free kick that floated towards goal like a falling leaf). The proudest exponents of the art in recent years must be Manchester United's Wayne Rooney, Zidane (outrageously, in the final of the 2006 World Cup) and Francesco Totti, Roma's captain and Italy's chief pin-up. Totti has regularly delighted in releasing the chip in the most audacious circumstances, most notably during a penalty shootout against Holland in the Euro 2000 tournament. Rooney, Zidane, Totti and Kavindele knew much of what fun in football was about; it was needed to mock any occasion that had grown too big for its boots.

But fun in football's about a little more than mockery, and one of England's greatest talents knew this all too well. In his autobiography, Paul Gascoigne mourns the end of England's campaign at the 1990 World Cup in Italy. 'Losing the semi', he wrote, 'was not the only reason for my tears. I was also crying because it was the end of the tournament for us, the end of those terrific six weeks or so in our World Cup camp. I didn't want to go home. I wanted to stay in the World Cup finals for ever. That would have suited me champion. So the realisation that all this was over was deeply depressing. I was wondering whether I would ever have this sort of fun again in my whole life. The suspicion that I wouldn't made me cry even more.'

There was Paul Gascoigne, afraid that he'd have to face real life; and, like Jimi Hendrix's joker, searching for 'some kind of way out of here'. Football provides escapism for players even more than it does for spectators, immersing them in a world where their eccentricities are at worst forgiven and celebrated at best. Gascoigne wasn't the first footballer to use the goldfish bowl of professional football as a hiding place, but he's probably the most famous. There are, broadly speaking, two popular views on his career, which seem, at first glance, to be wildly opposing.

One of them, expressed as a furious epitaph by Ian Wooldridge in the *Daily Mail*, is that 'he's a fat, ill-mannered Geordie who has urinated a glorious God-given talent against numerous walls.' The other is that Gascoigne, given his hyperactive and hypersensitive personality, achieved all that he reasonably could. Wooldridge could have gone easier on the venom, but both viewpoints are essentially true. The very best players in the game have been able to turn their capacity for fun on and off, but Gascoigne was always compelled to leave the tap running. Any assessment of his career must feature the words of the unfortunate spokesman at the Chinese second-division club where, just as he had at Lazio, Gascoigne spent an all too brief period. Despairing of Gascoigne's constant resort to pranks, he mumbled an exhausted explanation of why things had not worked out for the player at Gansu Tianma: 'Too much funny'.

Thanks to an autobiography of touching, often uncomfortable honesty, we now know that Gascoigne had an addictive personality, his addiction to fun on the pitch having been replaced by another, more damaging fixation. As he told *The Guardian*, 'On the football pitch I was a genius yet sometimes I did crazy things because all I ever thought about was football. That's why I began drinking – it helped take my mind off football.' Whilst Gascoigne carried his love affair with the game to extremes, other players drifted into apathy, due to the sustained torrent of cash into English football. At the turn of 2002, Arsène Wenger spoke warily of this trend, fearing that it would give the players different motivations. He said that 'my main concern is that what should make the big player today is, first, a love of the game.' Thankfully, Wenger didn't have to look far for reassurance. His star striker, Thierry Henry, had what his manager would describe as a healthy obsession with the sport, made clear by an interview with Bryan Appleyard in *The Sunday Times*:

His wife is said to get angry with the way he has to have a ball to play with at all times and one, I note, has been provided at our photo shoot. Football is the key aspect of his self-containment, it is the vessel in which he lives and breathes. He does not seem to need more.

For players such as Henry, though, the pleasure that they derive from football isn't rooted in escapism, as it was in Gascoigne's case. The pitch isn't some comfortable hospice where they go to make sense of the world; it's a place where the joy in their play is tightly wedded to their egos, and real delight is taken in the humiliation of an opponent. Witness the Premiership match against Tottenham Hotspur when Henry flicked the ball up in midfield and, juggling it as he jogged, made it halfway across the pitch before laying it off; or the Carling Cup final in 2006, when Manchester United's Cristiano Ronaldo performed the same insolent act against Wigan. In fact, Ronaldo's performance that day was one of the most contemptuous seen in English football since Leeds beat Southampton 7–0 in the league in 1972. On that day at Elland Road, Leeds scored a seventh and then indulged in a series of extravagant flicks and back-heels, keeping the ball for what seemed minutes on end as the home crowd roared in lusty approval. The scene was reminiscent of an amphitheatre at the Games, when a gladiator was toying with some woefully mismatched foe. The commentator, the BBC's Barry Davies, referred to Leeds' treatment of Southampton as 'almost cruel', an assessment with which Billy Bremner, one of the away team's chief tormentors, would later ruefully agree.

This, then, is fun with a harder edge: what David Winner in *Brilliant Orange* described as 'the ultimate put-down, the ultimate, aggressive assertion of dominance': fun as a weapon. And it's a sword that's wielded by the very best. Henrik Larsson told *World Soccer* magazine of the happiness in Ronaldinho's game, saying that 'Ronaldinho is a guy who comes in every morning with a smile on his face. You just have to look at him to get happy. It is fantastic – to be under such pressure and still smile. He has fun when he plays football and that's great. That's why he can play as well as he does.' However, Thierry Henry was perhaps closer to the Brazilian's true intentions when he said that 'all the time people talk about Ronaldinho smiling. I can tell you that inside there are no smiles.' As Henry implied, there's a cruelty in Ronaldinho's football, which you notice as soon as you remember that innocent children aren't the only animals that walk around with large, toothy grins; hyenas do that, too.

What Ronaldinho shares with Gascoigne, Rabah Madjer, and Jimi Hendrix's joker and the thief is a belief that, to quote the eighteenth-century actor David Garrick, 'comedy is a serious business'. To that end, he's among the most recent of a line of characters who go back thousands of years, long before anyone ever thought of inflating a pig's bladder and kicking it about: he has the spirit of Trickster, a proudly subversive character who gets his way through sly and often entertaining schemes. Trickster exists in Native American folk tales, in the form of the coyote, and in the myths of ancient Greece, where Prometheus deceived the gods by stealing fire from them and giving it to humans. Thanks to players like Rijkaard and Yorke, their tradition is alive and well in the new folk tales that football produces each season.

Trickster isn't to be confused, however, with the 'show-pony', that character who, like Verón too often in his career, is flamboyant for the sake of flamboyancy. In a sense, John Collins drew a distinction between the mere show-pony and Trickster. He spoke to me disparagingly of 'tricks', shows of skill that footballers put on during games, which looked good but never actually helped them to dribble past defenders. Real players like Henry and Zidane, he said, used effective pieces of skill, which would cause the opposition genuine problems: they used 'moves'. Trickster uses moves.

To play like Trickster, therefore, is no mean feat; it's almost a calling. As Lewis Hyde wrote in his seminal work in this field, *Trickster Makes this World*, 'Most of the travellers, liars, thieves, and shameless personalities of the twentieth century are not tricksters at all, then. Their disruptions are not subtle enough, or pitched at a high enough level. Trickster isn't a run-of-the-mill liar or thief. When he lies and steals, it isn't so much to get away with something or get rich as to disturb the established categories of truth and property and, by so doing, open the road to possible new worlds.'

It's remarkable how many of these footballers who open such roads don't look like footballers at all; it's as if their very appearances are part of the guile with which they operate on the pitch. Zinedine Zidane, with his bashful shuffle and hairline in rapid recession, looked like a bank clerk who'd lost his way home; Ferenc Puskás, of merrily plump cheeks and portly swagger, resembled a jovial train conductor. But the most mischievous of them all – and therefore the one who was visually the most unusual – was Garrincha, Brazil's brilliant winger of that country's triumph in the 1958 and 1962 World Cups. In Ruy Castro's book about him, which is not so much a biography as an often moving and reverent tribute, we find the following description:

> Garrincha didn't so much walk as sway… he was five-foot-six-and-a-half tall and weighed ten-and-a-half stone. His right knee bent inwards, his left knee bent outwards and he had a dislocated hip. According to the club doctors, his left leg was more than two inches shorter than his right, and depending on the angle of vision, one could see he was slightly cross-eyed.

It was Ruud Gullit, whilst working as a BBC commentator, who first uttered the phrase 'sexy football', but it was Garrincha who typified it, his play filled with ceaseless invention. Notably, the close connection between Garrincha's athletic performance and his sexual exuberance is one that Ruy Castro is delighted to maintain, and he even devotes an entire chapter of *Garrincha* to this theme. That chapter's name, 'Sex Machine', suggests an author rendered almost breathless by Garrincha's carnal aplomb, and its content confirms that suspicion. As Castro tells us, 'He was a machine who would do it any place, any time, with anyone … One local beauty, an actress, hosted *feijoadas* for the visiting players, and she, along with her equally attractive friend, was as tasty as any black beans or rice. Garrincha's colleagues believe he tried out both of them during one *feijoada* party in 1960 … [he'd spend] nights at the local brothel, where on at least one occasion Garrincha had a thorough workout session with a brunette and a blonde in quick succession.'

Garrincha was equally quick-witted on the field. As Castro reports, full-backs would often ask for his mercy before the game, but he'd rarely show it, finding instead new ways to flummox them, some of them nonsensical. Brazil's Ronaldo has recalled one moment when the Botafogo star dribbled towards a defender, and then simply ran away without the ball, leaving it to roll for a teammate as the defender continued after him in fruitless and clueless pursuit.

But to leave the ball alone was a rarity for Garrincha. He referred to the football affectionately as 'my girl', and, indeed, treated her at times as would a jealous lover, in that he'd frequently refuse to share her with anyone else. George Best was also fond of this metaphor of ball-as-bedfellow, once remarking that 'I know it sounds daft, but I loved the feel of it. I used to hold it, look at it and think, "One day you'll do everything I'll tell you."' Best may have felt foolish, but the infatuation with football has gone to greater extremes than that. Hernan Crespo, bravely risking the wrath of his girlfriend, described his match-winning goal for AC Milan against Manchester United in the 2005 Champions League as 'like more than an orgasm. I've never experienced a feeling as strong as that in the whole of my career. I really still can't explain what it felt like, scoring that goal. It helped show English supporters that I still exist.' But, not to be outdone, George Best had earlier raised the bar on this topic. For him, football wasn't, in some abstract sense, better than sex; it *was* sex. He once confessed to high excitement in his loins as he stepped onto the pitch. 'I noticed that when I touched the ball on the field', he said, 'you could hear this shrill noise in the crowd with all the birds screaming like at a Beatles concert … with the crowd cheering, I used to get the horn. Honestly. It used to arouse me, excite me. I felt the same way every time I walked onto the field at the start of a game.'

So it was with these grand notions of fun, stretching from Best and Garrincha back through time to Gordian knots and tricksters, that I asked the public what they thought: whether they felt that a great footballer needed a sense of fun. For this perceived quality, I met perhaps the broadest spread of views anywhere in the survey; about as many thought it an essential element as found it frivolous. Those who approved of its inclusion simply ranked it almost as highly as vision, and left it at that. But those who disapproved were a little more vocal.

Most sharp, and most succinct, was Fergus Eckersley: he observed that 'I play with a sense of fun. So does my dog.' Mark Smith felt that I should have used the category of 'passion' instead, which would have captured both the will to win and an enjoyment of the game. 'Fun seems vague', he wrote. 'Ronaldinho plays for the love of it with loads of tricks but generally in the opposition half. Joe Cole used to have tricks everywhere and was seen as a liability.' Steve Jeffes, tongue tucked in cheek – I hope – admonished me for my selection. 'Fun?', he asked incredulously. 'Fun is seeing your mate drop his Pukka pie down his fresh, clean shirt and having nothing to wipe it up with … There's no fun for footballers. They're essentially being fed to the lions every week for a lion's share of the wages.'

Jeffes was probably only half joking, and – from Roy Keane's point of view – he was entirely correct. Keane, in his autobiography, gave something of a painful perspective on professional football, his relationship with the sport reading like a loveless marriage. Keane wrote of his 'fear of failure', which was only exorcised by the arrival of success. He also revealed that 'I don't play football to be famous or celebrated, none of us does. Happiness is satisfying the demands of your business, repaying the fans' devotion, justifying your wages … Happiness is not being afraid.' From these analyses, there was little room for fun anywhere in football, which I found baffling, since football, after all, was a game, and to my mind fun and games went together as naturally as fish and chips.

But to talk of fun was almost sacrilegious; it was to make a jibe at the earnest dreams and anguish of supporters. In *Psycho*, Stuart Pearce gave short shrift to a former teammate who'd taken such an approach. He recalled that 'Gary Lineker made a statement when he retired saying that he had more important things in his life – his wife and his family – and that football was just something he had done. I am not like that at all.' Pearce's tone was almost one of outrage. 'I find that attitude as alien as probably he finds mine of football being something far more than just a game that you play for fun … Anyway, I'm not sure I totally believed Gary. He loved the game.'

I wanted an insider's view on how much – or how little – fun the modern footballer was having, and so one lunch break I took the Tube across town to speak with Andy Barton of the Sporting Mind clinic. Barton worked with athletes across the board, including Premiership footballers, and was a Trainer and Master Practitioner in Neuro-Linguistic Programming. (Which, as he helpfully translated that opaque title, meant that he was a sports pyschologist.)

His experience was that this love of the game was being squeezed out of players at an ever earlier stage. 'I get eleven-year-old kids in here who are from academies – and they may be from Chelsea, Arsenal, from Brentford, whoever they're with – and they have lost something by being in these academies', he told me. 'They're losing their sense of fun and enjoyment, and they've gained a sense of fear, because their fear is of whether or not they're going to make it through the next year. So their mind goes from being this ten-year-old who's carefree – trusting their instincts, beating every player there is in sight, passing fantastic passes, scoring fantastic goals – to being one going, "Oh God, I don't want to miss this tackle, I don't want to mess up this pass, I don't want to screw up, I don't want to look an idiot in front of my manager."'.

I suggested that Ronaldinho's smile was an emblem of his brilliance – that, as Henrik Larsson had noted, he managed to enjoy himself whilst (or perhaps because) the pressure was at its greatest. Barton thought that the issue went deeper than that. 'One of the first things I work with people on is getting their enjoyment back', he said. 'Because – as in all professions – there comes a point where they think they have to take it seriously, and [that] being serious means being down on yourself, beating yourself up, being hypercritical. So you lose your carefree element because, well, if I'm being carefree I'm not taking this seriously enough, and this can't be important enough, and I can't do it properly. But actually, by staying carefree, you can be the Frank Lampard or the Steven Gerrard who takes a penalty for Chelsea or Liverpool, as opposed to the different people that they almost are [when playing] for England when they walk towards that penalty spot with their hearts pumping, with their Bambi eyes caught in the car's headlights.'

Simon Barnes was of a similar mind. In *The Meaning of Sport*, he observed that 'commentators say again and again: "And now it's all about who wants it more." Actually, the victory can often go to the one who wants it less: the one who can take the competition in their stride, with relaxed muscles and mind. The one who thinks it really is life and death can get consumed by the madness of the occasion.' To shed further light on this point Barnes went on to quote Ed Smith, the Middlesex cricketer, who's written that "It's the easiest criticism of all. He lost concentration on that four-foot putt, people say, as though it's like forgetting to lock your car door. Just a lack of attention. Sometimes it is, but how much more often is failure the result of trying too hard, of tensing up, of over-revving. Most sportsmen try too hard, not too little."'

When discussing the Italians' approach to professional football, Arsène Wenger was of the same school of thought as Ed Smith. As he told Vialli and Marcotti in *The Italian Job*, 'In Italy, football is no longer a sport, it's a job, an industry. You have lost something, you are too severe, the players don't enjoy themselves any more. It's rare to see an Italian player smiling in training or on the pitch. He is totally focused and concentrated and he can't think of anything else. In England, they laugh, they have fun and they still give a hundred per cent. You only need to look at the environment in the dressing room before a match. In Italy or France they are tense, they are fully concentrated on the game, they are thinking about what they need to do. In England, it's like a discothèque. There is music, fun, chaos.'

So football life was all smiles in England, and hellish in Italy, as Wenger noted anecdotally; but I had to take his comments as being some way off the mark, given the heated English responses to my survey. In its own way, English football is just as serious as its Continental version. For one, the legendary Liverpool manager Bill Shankly is widely quoted as seeing the game as more important than life and death. From most mouths, you'd immediately dismiss a statement like that as tongue-in-cheek, but the Scot was so intensely focused on winning that he might actually have meant it. So, thanks to Shankly's passion, I needed to look at what science had to say.

So, was football fun, or more likely to be fatal? Witte, Bots, Hoes and Grobbee had had a paper published in the *British Medical Journal* in December 2000, entitled 'Cardiovascular mortality in Dutch men during 1996 European football championship.' For this piece of research, they'd analysed the effect of the Dutch team's performance on their fans, and they'd found that 'important sporting events may provoke a sufficient level of stress to trigger symptomatic cardiovascular disease.' The important sporting event to which they referred in this case was the quarter-final between Holland and France on 22 June, which was watched by approximately 9.8 million people, or over 60% of the Dutch population. Holland had lost that match on penalties – an outcome that their national side have achieved with a consistency almost as impressive as that of England – and Witte et al. revealed that 'compared with the average mortality in the preceding and following days, about fourteen additional events occurred; this is an increase of around 50%'.

This was an eye-catching increase, so I read on. The paper also stated that 'no corresponding increase in mortality occurred in women'. Without wanting to slip, as had Wenger, into the straitjacket of stereotype, I was tempted to conclude that maybe women just didn't care so much. This suspicion grew when I found that, out of the hundreds to whom I'd sent it, only one woman had responded to my questionnaire. However, Emma Furlong's comments showed as much indignation as any answer that I was to receive. 'I know we all have differing opinions about football but I find some of your choices bewildering', she wrote, before signing off loudly, 'TOON ARMY FOREVER'. As Furlong's example taught me not to be narrow-minded, so did the Dutchmen who'd suffered fatal heart complications; so often they're stereotyped as a laid-back race, but that laconic façade slips swiftly aside when Holland are playing.

Witte et al. also noted that 'the finding of increased risks of cardiovascular events during earthquakes and wars has provided strong support for a triggering role of emotional and mental stress. Our findings show that an important football match can similarly provide sufficient triggers to cause a rise in mortality from myocardial infarction (heart attack) and stroke.' The wars to which Witte et al. referred were the first Gulf War, and the mid-1990s conflict in Zagreb; and now men living in far more peaceful climates were, quite literally, worrying themselves to death over football.

But before I leapt to any moralistic conclusions as to why we men should bother ourselves with far higher concerns than the Beautiful Game, I had to consider the views of the French researchers Toubiana, Hanslik and Letrilliart. They'd cast significant doubt on the findings of Witte et al. by asking how many of those forty-one reported Dutch fatalities had actually been watching the game. This was a fair observation, and their rebuttal seemed promising; their research, conducted in France at the same time as Witte et al had carried out their study, showed that the mortality rate of French citizens hadn't been affected during that period. (Then again, the French *had* won the shootout.)

So, after all, it was unclear whether Frenchmen were hardier souls than Dutchmen. As the studies showed, French women, like their Dutch counterparts, remained untroubled by the match's result, probably rolling their eyes with equal disapproval at the fuss that the lads were making. And why did those lads – fans, players and managers alike – put themselves through it? In case there was any doubt about the adverse effects of watching football on supporters' health, it was put emphatically to rest by Kirkup and Merrick in their 2003 paper, *A matter of life and death: population mortality and football results*. Analysing the connection between poor results for football teams in north-east England and heart attacks in the same region, the two researchers produced a passage that was hard not to view as a smoking gun. 'In Sunderland Health Authority', they observed, 'stroke and acute myocardial infarction deaths increased by 66% in men on days when Sunderland AFC lost at home and this difference was significant. Across the four areas combined (total resident population just over two million), male deaths increased by 30% when the local professional football team lost at home and this difference is highly unlikely to be attributable to chance alone.'

What's more, these startling statistics were recorded before Sunderland AFC embarked on the most horrific Premiership season that any team has so far endured: in the 2005–6 season they were relegated with just fifteen points and only one home win, which surpassed the previous low that they themselves had set in the 2002–3 relegation season. The hope is that long-suffering Sunderland fans developed, over time, the strength of heart to withstand such constant strain; in any event, Kirkup and Merrick didn't publish an updated report to take account of this team's second relegation, perhaps feeling that it would have been too morbid to do so.

I wrote earlier of Paul Gascoigne finding escapism in football, but I'd thought that the definition of escape was to remove yourself from a threat to your health, not to leap headlong into one. But escape isn't that straightforward a concept. Yi-Fu Tuan, who has penned the leading work on this theme – titled, inevitably, *Escapism* – gave a sharp analysis of why the loyal supporter suffers as much as he does. 'Human vulnerability is not only a subjection to physical pain, disablement and death', wrote Tuan. 'It is also a corrosive sense of emptiness at the core of being, which one tries to overcome with the drowsing fumes of alcohol or drugs, and with socially approved work, projects, entertainments, but above all with human company, the hum of small talk that plugs every opening to ominous silence. We need other people, then, not just as a bulwark against external threat but as an effective diversion from having to confront this inner vacuity.'

Or, put simply, misery loves company. What those fans were doing, then, was escaping their loneliness by finding a communal activity in which they could lose themselves, although you suspect that they could've found a more joyful pursuit than following Sunderland AFC at the tail-end of Mick McCarthy's tenure. You also have to wonder whether watching a slow and sombre relegation qualifies, in Tuan's eyes, as 'socially approved entertainment'. Tuan, a retired professor emeritus in geography at the University of Wisconsin, was most likely unaware of the complexities of life at the base of the Premiership, but his words are of surprisingly suitable application. He wasn't talking in the following quote about the danger of becoming absorbed in your team's plight, but he might as well have been: 'Fantasy that is shut off too long from external reality risks degenerating into a self-deluding hell', he thought, 'a hell that can nevertheless have an insidious appeal'. And when he dismissed theme parks as 'escapist fantasies, suitable only for the immature', he could have written off football stadiums with equal disdain.

Tuan could also have been talking about Brazil's training sessions in preparation for the 2006 World Cup. Fun, as we've discussed, is a useful technique; not only does it relax footballers in stressful times, allowing them to express themselves without excessive tension, but it also intimidates the opposition to see a team perform so well without apparent effort. But there's a line beyond which football becomes frivolous, and Brazil crossed it that summer in Germany. Nigel Adderley, a Radio Five Live correspondent, writing on the BBC's World Cup blog, thus described the scenes from Brazil's final practice at Berlin's Olympic Stadium before their opening game against Croatia:

> It was a chaotic circus which was high on flair and low on any sort of organisation. In a fantastically entertaining kick-about, Ronaldo (not as fat as you may believe) played in a holding midfield role while goalkeeper Dida put himself about up front and knocked in a couple of very tidy goals. It may have been for the benefit of the hundreds of watching media but this bore no relation to how they will line up against Croatia and the wild celebrations when anyone scored were massively over the top – but it was great fun which may be the point.

There was an irony in Adderley's account that didn't fully emerge until Brazil were eliminated by France. That is to say, that the side that Brazil fielded against Croatia and on through the tournament bore every relation to the line-up that Adderley had seen in their training session: haphazard, with Ronaldinho's deep-lying role effectively that of a holding midfielder, and, worse still, seemingly half-hearted. Steve McManaman would have known more about the Brazilian mentality than most, having played with Roberto Carlos and Ronaldo at Real Madrid, so I made a point of asking him about this issue when I spoke with him. We met in a Soho bar on a Friday afternoon; I had sidled my way through a typically congested Oxford Street, whilst he had travelled down south with Rob Jones, a close friend and former teammate from his Liverpool days.

He and Jones, as McManaman was quick to observe, represented opposite sides of luck's coin. McManaman had suffered sustained injury only at the end of his career, in his two-year spell at Manchester City; Jones, however, had had a rougher time of things, leaving the game at the age of twenty-eight due to recurring problems with his left knee. Jamie Carragher – perhaps with a helping of Liverpudlian bias – had thought him a superior player to Gary Neville, believing that he'd have gone on to be capped seventy or eighty times for England, had selection and good health gone his way. And if that assessment of Jones' qualities seems somewhat partisan, then there's the following anecdote, related by Steve Hunter for Liverpool's selection of *100 Players Who Shook the Kop*:

Rob Jones, brought in from Crewe Alexandra, [was] plunged into a debut at a high-profile ground, Old Trafford; playing against Ryan Giggs who was at the top of his form at [that] moment, the most feared left-winger in Europe… and Rob Jones was absolutely brilliant. He marked Ryan Giggs out of the game.

Hunter recalled a programme that BBC's Newsround had run a few weeks after that game, where:

a few of the kids were asking Ryan Giggs some questions. And they asked him, "Who's your most feared opponent, Ryan?" And he said, "Without question, Rob Jones of Liverpool. I can never get the better of him."

Jones agreed with the above assessment; he'd not found Giggs too worrying a proposition, with the Frenchman David Ginola instead being his least favourite opponent. As for McManaman, he'd introduced himself with the words, 'Hi, I'm Steven', modestly not assuming that I'd been obsessively watching the UEFA Champions League for the last few years, which of course I had. Since he'd left Madrid, it seemed that he'd been on something of a glorified gap year, having travelled to various parts of the Middle and Far East. What's more, he and his wife Victoria had recently had their first child, and if anything was going to rattle McManaman's famously relaxed cage, it was being woken up at 3 a.m. by a wailing new arrival.

McManaman was keen to discuss Brazil's behaviour at the 2006 World Cup. It turned out that he, Nigel Adderley and I had been watching their preparation with equal bemusement. 'Open training sessions are a nonsense', said McManaman, 'because half the time it's for the punters that come in, but they were probably like that [all the time] because they approached every game in the same way. Whether it's worked for them in the past and they think they can get away with it, I don't know, but they approached it in a very light-hearted way.'

Brazil and France had of course met in the quarter-final of that tournament, with the French emerging victorious. This was less surprising given the contrast in their playing styles, the Brazilians often more determined to use a trick for its own sake, while the French used flamboyance to a more decisive end. At some level, you could scarcely blame the Brazilians for their wastefulness; with that much technique at their disposal, it must have been tempting for them to fool around with the ball almost all the time. Had there been frequent showboating sessions during training at Real Madrid, I wondered. 'Yeah, all the time', said McManaman. 'Every day. Roberto Carlos, Ronaldo... every single day. The Brazilians liked to express themselves, and they were quite loud, always laughing and joking.' And Zidane? McManaman's answer was telling: 'Whereas the Brazilians did it more to get attention, he did it without meaning to do it, without thinking... he wasn't necessarily showing off. It was just part of his game.'

Zidane, then, was Trickster incarnate, which won't be news to anyone who saw him in action; he'd managed to harness his limitless talent, and that of the team around him, to an effective end that Brazil would have done well to note. But the pragmatic nature of his play wasn't lost on Maradona, who'd previously criticised both him and Michel Platini for their approach to the game. In *El Diego*, he'd written of Zidane that 'I want to defend him, because he has such extraordinary vision, but he looks to me as if he feels less like playing every day that goes by. He's just like Platini: he doesn't have fun. They both lack joy when they play.' In marked contrast, he praised the work of Alessandro del Piero, describing him as 'the opposite of Zidane: he likes to play, he feels it in his soul. Between him and the French guy, I choose this one.'

That's probably unfair of Maradona, but he wouldn't have been the first to claim to know the deepest recesses of Zidane's mind. It's very easy for both players and sportswriters to claim to know the workings of the Frenchman's inner room – and I may have fallen into that trap in my discussion, still to come, of Madness – but for now I was still keen to analyse Brazil's attempt to turn the 2006 World Cup into a carnival. As McManaman recalled of their selection policy, 'They put the big names in for fear of upsetting them, didn't they? They all played.'

'They' were Brazil's so-called Magic Quartet, the diverse and mercurial creative line of Ronaldinho, Ronaldo, Kaká and Adriano: their collective name gave them a dignity which masked the orgy of formlessness that they ultimately produced. As McManaman observed, 'I went over to watch the Brazil–Australia game, and you think to yourself, well, they can't all play, because it's impossible. They cannot all play. And then suddenly they all played and you think, where are they all going to play?' Anywhere and everywhere, as it turned out: 'Ronaldinho was playing in centre midfield, and he was ineffective, and Kaká was over there, and he was ineffective, and Ze Roberto, and Ronnie ... and they were all over the place. It was a shambles.'

The inevitable contrast arises between Brazil's conduct at the 2006 World Cup and that of their footballing ancestors at the World Cup in 1970, who, though more gifted, showed far less vanity in their outlook. That 1970 side, one of the best-loved in any sport, had men of greater guile than the Magic Quartet and their colleagues. Indeed, in Tostão,

Rivellino, Jarzinho and Pelé, they had had a Magic Quartet of their own. Moreover, where the 2006 edition could only boast Ze Roberto, a converted left-winger, as their defensive axis in midfield, the class of 1970 had the 'hard-as-bell-metal' Gérson, who in Hugh McIlvanney's view was the true heart of this magnificent team. But in 1970, that victorious eleven made sacrifices for each other all over the pitch, typified by Clodoaldo in defensive midfield, who, though he had the ability to beat several men in a single dribble, restrained himself to one or two touches at a time.

That wasn't the case with the 2006 version, of whom Simon Kuper wrote damningly in *The Financial Times* that:

This is not a team. When asked about Brazil's strengths, Juninho Pernambucano didn't give the ritual answer of 'the collective', but said: 'Our individuals' ... A German observer of their 3–0 victory over Ghana described the Brazilians as 'Harlem Globetrotters who have forgotten to go to Weight Watchers' ... Cafu is 36, seldom reaches the byline any longer, was repeatedly bamboozled by Croatia's Dado Prso, and after a sprint in the last minute against Ghana lay down on the grass as if to nap. The 33-year-old Roberto Carlos springs to life only when Brazil get a free kick – the old man's refuge – which he ritually blasts into space. But he is a luxury Brazil can afford. They could win a second straight World Cup playing at half-cock.

Thankfully, they didn't; where the 1970 team arguably differed from the pretenders of 2006 was in their ability to take the game with a lightness of touch that didn't descend into whimsy. The hubris of Brazil's 2006 campaign found its symbol in the absurd headband, emblazoned with a bright gold 'R', that Ronaldinho wore against France. The thinking here was clearly that once the defending champions had disposed of the Gauls, Ronaldinho's fashion item would result in a windfall for both him and his sponsors. Of course, there was the small matter of first defeating a French playmaker whose greatness was already long beyond dispute; having realised this, the shamefaced Ronaldinho emerged for the second half of the quarter-final with the headband nowhere to be seen.

Yet when I suggested to Simon Barnes that the great players needed – within the limits of vanity – to have a sense of fun, he wasn't so sure. He felt that they enjoyed the game 'only incidentally... I don't think anyone would say Franz Beckenbauer was characterised by a sense of fun in what he did, there was a grimness of purpose in his play.' By the same token, Barnes had described the beauty of Roger Federer's tennis as being a mere by-product of the Swiss champion's success. 'Roger Federer is not an artist', wrote Barnes, 'he is a businessman. He does not seek to beguile our senses or to make us sigh with pleasure. He is just a man looking for the best method to win tennis matches. Yet for some reason this method is sublimely beautiful. Federer is no more seeking to create beauty when he plays tennis than a cheetah is trying to create beauty when he pursues a gazelle.'

What was going on here, I wondered. What was wrong with people? I'd always seen fun as both a crucial form of release and of self-expression for the great footballer, but it looked as if I was in the minority here. The majority of respondents to my survey seemed to view the game with as much joy as they did the completion of a tax return, whilst Zidane and Federer played the game with an apologetic beauty. It made me wonder what people really meant when they said that they loved football. How could you profess passion for a sport if you couldn't revel in its beauty, if you were so absorbed in your pursuit of victory that you didn't stop to dwell on the vignettes of skill that litter every good game?

Yes, football was life and death, blood and sweat and so on. But, as I asked Steve McManaman, when all was said and done, it was a laugh, wasn't it? Wasn't it? 'Every day you're training, and you do have a great time, joking and skitting on people', said McManaman. (Reassuringly.) 'I mean, we went to work with twenty lads, and played football. Of course, there were various tasks at various times, but in the end you're messing about with twenty people who you live with and see more than your wife. Of course there's a lot of pressure on the Saturday when you play, but that's what it's all about, isn't it? It's the best job in the world.'

Endurance

Running clean, clever lines towards goal, three games a week, week in, week out, year on year upon year, he played at the top level until his late thirties, often performing round trips of the country as he went...

The above description is half-paraphrased, half-plagiarised, from *White Storm*, Phil Ball's fine history of Real Madrid. The player in question is Alfredo di Stefano, or the Blond Arrow, a man around whom there's a curious, collective mental block whenever people are naming the greatest footballers of all time. Once Pelé, Maradona and various mangled pronunciations of Cruyff have spilled from many mouths, di Stefano will typically be mentioned as an afterthought, a little like the lonely and grumpy uncle whom you feel obliged to invite to Christmas lunch. And that's unfair on the Argentine. 'Superbly versatile, endlessly energetic, forever domineering' were Brian Glanville's words about him in *The Times*, testament to a man involved centrally in five consecutive European Cup triumphs in the 1950s, and various other national championships besides. Di Stefano set goalscoring records in Europe that took three decades to break, and others that will remain comfortably untouched. Yet there remains this lack of warmth, this slow endorsement of di Stefano's deeds.

Part of that can be put down to the fact that his career preceded, albeit by only a decade, the true advent of televised sport. Portugal's Eusebio, a lesser light, received greater exposure for his exploits in the 1960s, as did George Best. But that can't be the only reason. Ferenc Puskás, the rotund Hungarian, who was the Blond Arrow's partner up front for many years, is remembered affectionately both for his portly posture, and for his masterclass in a 6–3 defeat of England at Wembley. Maybe di Stefano's been taken for granted for so long because he simply endured. There's no distinctive technique or skill that he could call his own, no flourish of vanity that he pioneered. None of the shots that he fired wasted any time on their way to the net; they speared in at the near post, they didn't waft in upon the wind like some Roberto Baggio free kick, soaring gracefully into the far corner. Di Stefano's entire career was an ode to good geometry, to plain, precise angles of passing and shooting.

This quiet but formidable accumulation of goals and trophies was something that di Stefano shared with Raúl, a later Madrid legend who was to be similarly maligned. Good geometry, as a rule, doesn't really stir hearts or imaginations; but to produce it for hundreds of games in succession is a great virtue, and should be celebrated as such. In this area, American sport sets an excellent example. Lou Gehrig, a star first-baseman for the New York Yankees, played 2,130 consecutive games for his team over a fourteen-year period between 1925 and 1939. This record, remarkably, was broken by Cal Ripken Jr of the Baltimore Orioles in 1995, and Ripken's record playing streak has been christened – somewhat unimaginatively – The Streak.

In fairness to football, player loyalty is something to which fans have generally responded well. Of course, it makes it easier if the loyal player is as relentlessly brilliant as di Stefano, but the flip side of their affection is the contempt that's often bred by familiarity. For a case study, we needn't look further than the treatment of Alessandro del Piero by Juventus in 2005. Del Piero, although the club captain, was substituted over twenty times that season; this repeated humiliation had no real logic to support it, unless perhaps it was a year-long process of iconoclasm by the then coach Fabio Capello. In the annals of Italian football, with its chorus of extroverts, del Piero's understated manner ran contrary to the wanton flamboyance of so many lesser stars; but he seemed, at times, to attract more hostility than any of the game's villains. Lazio's Paolo di Canio and Siniša Mihajlović were both briefly excoriated by the media for their proud connections to, respectively, a Fascist organisation and a Serbian warlord. However, in a classic demonstration of football's skewed priorities, del Piero was pilloried ceaselessly for a season of poor form, at the end of which he revealed with a quiet dignity that his father was dying of cancer, but he hadn't wished to use this private tragedy as an excuse during the league campaign.

Del Piero's difficult relationship with the press had begun some seasons before that, when he became the scapegoat for Italy's failure to win the European Championship in 2000. That year, they'd faced France in the final, and as a late substitute he'd missed two excellent opportunities with the score at 1–0 to Italy. France went on to win 2–1 with a golden goal from Trezeguet; never mind that Toldo had allowed a last-minute equaliser from Wiltord to slip under his body, or that Italy collectively were at fault for losing concentration so late in the match. It was del Piero who carried the can for years, and who became a convenient focus for the public's discontent. To endure the world of football and the host of capricious souls who dwell there, is therefore no mean feat. Fans, be they in the stands or the boardroom, are often impatient not only for success but also for change for the sake of change. Witness the smugly-silent atmospheres at clubs whose crowds have become accustomed to their winning, week in, week out: Highbury was often referred to as 'the Library' due to the bookish timidity and relative silence of its fans while Arsenal conquered all at the turn of this new century, whilst in the late 1990s del Piero's home ground, the Stadio delle Alpi, had a similarly complacent crowd. What, then, gives these footballers the ability to last as long as they do at the peak of their sport?

'The people who tend be most successful are the ones who are good at setting goals for themselves', Andy Barton told me. 'A really good example is Frank Lampard, who, if you notice from the point he joined Chelsea as a good player, has improved year on year on year, to the point where he's world-class. You can only do that if you've set your sights on improving, which is an underestimated area.' He likened Lampard's training regime, and subsequent progress, to the yield that a banker might make on a shrewd investment plan. But what made Lampard a Premiership winner was, of course, more than the cumulative effect of a series of weights sessions. It was a question of want, upon which Muhammad Ali, as upon most other issues, has been eloquent. 'Champions aren't made in gyms', he once said. 'Champions are made from something they have deep inside them – a desire, a dream, a vision. They have to have last-minute stamina, they have to be a little faster, they have to have the skill and the will. But the will must be stronger than the skill.'

Kevin Keegan, in his time at Liverpool and then Hamburg SV in the early 1970s and late 1980s, had limitless will; and just as well, as a cynic might retort, since he didn't have the casual grace of many other Anfield strikers. Yet, on an individual basis, he was more successful than Michael Owen, Robbie Fowler or Ian Rush. His application saw him twice receive the *Ballon d'Or* as European Footballer of the Year, and he's still the only Englishman to have achieved this feat. Michel Platini was another multiple winner of this accolade; in his Juventus days he was the only player to have taken the Golden Ball home three years in a row, between 1984 and 1986, a record that still stands. In a poll by French sports publication *L'Équipe*, he was also voted French footballer of the century ahead of Zinedine Zidane and Raymond Kopa, a contemporary of di Stefano during Real Madrid's period of utter dominance. Not content with recognition on that scale, Platini has spoken uncharitably of Zidane's talents, saying that 'Zidane does some extraordinary things, it's true. But you have to put everything in context. What Zidane does with a ball, Maradona could do with an orange.'

Platini's apparent bitterness shows that a sporting legend's work is never done. Years after leaving the pitch for the last time, Platini has continued to fight for his legacy in a fashion that, as Ronaldo once revealed to Brazilian newspaper *O Globo*, has caused Zidane to understand him as jealous. But Platini's comments weren't so much about Zidane as they were about Platini: he had fought for years to see that once he retired he'd be regarded as irrefutably the greatest, and all of a sudden Zidane, this North African via Marseilles, threatened to shake him free of the seat he thought he'd always occupy. In *Serious*, his autobiography, John McEnroe wrote of being in a similar predicament. 'I guess you could say that history, and whatever part I've been able to play in it, has always felt extremely important to me', he admitted. 'Like me, Andre Agassi has seven Grand Slam titles altogether; but unlike me, he's won all four of the majors, even if not in one calendar year. His place in history

is secure. Where does that leave me? I guess only time will tell ... '
McEnroe, although three times the champion of Wimbledon, then
speaks of an insecurity that haunts him, at times literally so. 'I'll confess
it', he writes, 'I feel I could have done more. There are nights when I
can't get to sleep for thinking about the Australian Opens I passed by
when I was at the peak of my game and always felt I'd have another
chance; the French Open that I had in the palm of my hand, then choked
away.'

That's the curse of the world-class sportsman: to complete his career,
fade from the immediate spotlight, and then wait anxiously to see
whether he'll be supplanted in the people's affections. What McEnroe
wanted was what Rod Laver possessed: 'a rock-solid claim to being one
of the greatest tennis players of all time'. Maybe his life would have been
a little easier if he'd learned how to relax. Seneca the Younger, the
Roman philosopher of the first century AD, came up with the quote
about all geniuses being touched by madness (of which, more later). But
he also wrote a passage asking obsessively successful souls like John
McEnroe – that is to say, all elite yet frustrated athletes – to be calm and
enjoy what they'd already achieved. 'We are plunged by our blind
desires', wrote Seneca, 'into ventures which will harm us, but certainly
will never satisfy us; for if we could be satisfied with anything, we should
have been satisfied long ago; nor do we reflect how pleasant it is to
demand nothing, how noble it is to be contented and not to be dependent upon Fortune. Therefore continually remind yourself... how many
ambitions you have attained. When you see many ahead of you, think
how many are behind you. If you would thank the gods, and be grateful
for your past life, you should contemplate how many men you have
outstripped. But what have you to do with the others? You have
outstripped yourself.'

Any footballer who truly wants to be great will have begun tearing the
above paragraph to pieces about halfway through. Because it's asking
them to settle meekly for second best, and that's something that they're
incapable of doing. As Vince Lombardi, the legendary American Football coach, once said: 'Show me a good loser, and I'll show you a loser.'

73

And that's what endurance, in this context, is all about: dragging, harassing yourself to new heights over the course of your sporting life, so that one day you'll be so firmly fixed in the pantheon of greats that no one will question your place. Such a position is occupied by Pelé, who in his retirement has the serenity of one who is truly untouchable.

Of course, if we're looking to hard fact to see who endured the longest, then we can't look any further than Pelé. Much – perhaps too much – has been said about his extraordinary achievements over an extraordinary period of time, to the extent that assertion of his greatness becomes somewhat stale. The numbers are mind-numbing, undulating towards you in wave after wave of monotonous brilliance: three World Cup winners' medals, in 1958, 1962 and 1970; 1282 goals in 1366 games; 635 goals in 648 domestic matches. These statistics are imposing and remote, a little like the words on your great-grandfather's gravestone; you know that you owe them respect, but it's impossible to relate to them. But I found some words that breathed life into these figures, and they came from a surprising source.

Dr Henry Kissinger – when not involved in morally dubious statecraft in Indonesia and Cambodia – penned an engaging essay about Pelé for *Time* magazine, the Brazilian being the only footballer to make that publication's list of the 100 People of the Century. The former US Secretary of State wrote that 'performance at a high level in any sport is to exceed the ordinary human scale. But Pelé's performance transcended that of the ordinary star by as much as the star exceeds ordinary performance.' That's partly because Pelé sat astride the sporting world for longer than anyone else, which is all the more remarkable for the fact that he was a striker. The chief asset of a forward is often his pace, and it's also the asset that's prone to the swiftest depreciation; it thus attests well to Pelé's longevity that, in his final season and aged thirty-six, he still averaged a goal every two games. Pelé completed his career for the New York Cosmos, and his 13 goals in 25 matches were vital in leading them to the North American Soccer League title in 1977. The sharp cultural contrast that Pelé provided – the god of football making his grand farewell in a land where gridiron was king – led Kissinger to reflect on the differences between American sport and the Beautiful Game. He considered that 'American team sports are more cerebral and require a degree of skill that is beyond the reach of the layman. Baseball, for instance, requires a bundle of disparate skills: hitting a ball thrown at 90 mph, catching a ball flying at the speed of a bullet, and throwing long distances with great accuracy.'

I bristled a little at Kissinger's description, although my reaction was a parochial one. The thought that the American athlete was somehow more enlightened didn't sit well with my ego, or with my view of football as a sport whose apparent ease was a mask of its infinite complexity. Expecting to be offended further, I read on:

> Football requires a different set of skills for each of its 11 positions. The US spectator thus finds himself viewing two discrete events: what is actually taking place on the playing field and the translation of it into detailed and minute statistics. He wants his team to win, but he is also committed to the statistical triumph of the star he admires.

Kissinger seemed to be writing about the split personality of the US sports fan: on one hand, lost in the moment, and on the other, rummaging carefully through reams of data. Even with the advent of ProZone and Carling Opta Statistics, organisations which provide the detailed analysis of player performance that many Americans might crave, it may be that football, as a sport, just doesn't generate enough numbers to grab wholesale attention in the United States. Kissinger would have had better first-hand experience of this obstacle than most, since it was he who was pivotal in bringing Pelé to New York to play for the Cosmos in the 1970s, and in helping the USA to win its bid for the 1994 World Cup.

Incidentally, whether football will ever take off in stateside affections – or, in a typically clunky phrase once uttered to me by a strategy consultant, 'get traction' – is currently still a moot point, even with David Beckham's move to the LA Galaxy. A televised poll that I saw when I was in Dallas for that aforementioned World Cup showed that only 29% of Americans realised that the World Cup was taking place in their country. I wasn't sure which was more revealing: the result of the survey, or the fact that someone even felt it necessary to conduct one. But whether football will endure in America is a debate for another time.

For now, we come back briefly to Kissinger's implication. If the rest of the football world isn't as obsessed with statistics as are its American followers, then maybe the length of an outstanding player's career isn't so important when assessing his greatness. My survey seemed to confirm this, with endurance lagging in fifth place. It can be strongly argued that Jim Baxter secured legendary status after only five superb seasons for Rangers and Scotland; and Hugh McIlvanney, interviewed by *The Independent*, declared Wayne Rooney 'incontrovertibly a great player' when Rooney was still only twenty. He also anointed a star of Celtic's 1967 European Cup triumph: 'A great player who'd a very short career was Bobby Murdoch', he said, 'but the reason he had a short career was his weight. [His manager] Jock Stein once said a lovely thing to me about Murdoch. He said: "We keep sending him down to the health farm at Tring, but all we get back are tips from bad jockeys!"'

There was even the romantic notion from Fergus Eckersley – who'd earlier had a good go at my thesis about Fun – that the shortness of a player's career could actually contribute to his greatness. For Eckersley, 'ephemeral beauty is sometimes more compelling' for the lack of endurance. There was something attractive in that view, of a player who'd flitted briefly but gloriously across the world stage; it made them more lovable somehow, like a passionate but futile long-distance fling. As McIlvanney also reminded me, Paddy Crerand, a teammate and close friend of George Best, once said that you'd only have to have seen Best play for twenty minutes to see that he was one of the game's legends.

Crerand was speaking truth in jest; a long and decorated career is one thing, but another kind of endurance – the vital kind, which ensures that your reputation resounds through the ages – is how firmly you grasp the emotions of those who watch you. And that explosive impression can be made at any point of your career. Michael Owen's strike against Argentina at the 1998 World Cup probably pushed him faster down the road towards greatness than any teenager has ever travelled; it propelled him even faster than Patrick Kluivert's European Cup-winning goal for Ajax in 1995 against AC Milan. But perhaps it didn't push Owen far enough; moments were the building blocks of greatness, but maybe more mortar was needed. 'I think [Paul] Gascoigne was almost all potential', McIlvanney told me, almost wistfully. 'Gascoigne didn't have one great season. The talent was indisputable, but he was so crazy in a kind of cheap way. Obviously Paul's daftness has tragic dimensions – it's a tragedy that he didn't do more, because he had a lot of ability – but he was just so cheaply superficial about everything he did, and that's the sadness.'

It's worth revisiting Gascoigne's career, since his claim for some kind of greatness is a compelling one. Although he lost his prime through injury, the portfolio that he put together was still very impressive. In 57 games for England, he finished on the losing side on only four occasions, and at Glasgow Rangers he was irrepressible, inspiring them to three Scottish Premier League titles. Though many might be scornful of football north of the border, it's worth noting that his displays there contributed to his inclusion, after the 2002 inaugural vote, in the National Hall of Fame. Maybe it's revealing that he arrived there before Gary Lineker, whose public image was infinitely more statesmanlike, and whose personal achievements were more numerous than Gascoigne's; Lineker had been voted the Football Writers' Association Player of the Year in 1986 and 1992, and received the ultimate accolade from his peers, the title of PFA Players' Player of the Year in 1986.

Lineker reached the Hall of Fame the year after Gascoigne. But, whilst Lineker's class-of-2003 contained a mixture of both artists (Danny Blanchflower) and artisans (Alan Ball), the original inductees, including Gascoigne, were figureheads almost to a man, the type of footballers around whom great teams were built. They were what, in football-speak, comprised the spine: men such as Sir Tom Finney, Johnny Haynes, Bobby Moore and Dave Mackay. For Gascoigne to be included among their number suggested that he'd converted more of that potential into reality than McIlvanney or I had given him credit; or maybe he'd been chosen not because of his trophies, but due to his uniquely magical style of play.

For Simon Barnes, mere beauty wouldn't have been good enough to get Gascoigne into that sort of firmament. As he'd written, a little unforgivingly, in *The Meaning of Sport*, 'Greatness … requires an aspect of longevity. It is not about one perfect performance or one perfect tournament, a single masterpiece. No: it is about the accumulation of an *oeuvre*. A life. A CV. A biography … ' Someone like Lothar Matthäus would have more easily satisfied Barnes' requirements; the German dutifully prolonged the stereotype of his nation's efficiency over a twenty-year career, performing with an almost matchless consistency. The only outfield player to appear at five World Cups, a midfield crusader for Internazionale and Bayern Munich, he either witnessed first-hand or acted directly in the moments that defined football in the 1980s and 1990s; when Barnes talked of an *oeuvre*, there thus couldn't have been one richer than his.

A series of snapshots taken throughout the career of Matthäus would have made for an engrossing photo album: there he'd be, grappling with Maradona, on whom he'd performed an ultimately unsuccessful man-marking job in the 1986 World Cup final; shell-shocked as Porto and Manchester United stole the European Cup from Bayern in 1987 and 1999; euphoric as he strutted through the streets of Milan, having brought the Italian championship, *lo scudetto*, to the San Siro in 1989. For good measure, Matthäus had also thrown in one of Barnes' 'perfect tournaments', in the form of his formidable showing at the World Cup in 1990. The captain of victorious West Germany (as it then was), he scored four goals to ensure his side's passage to the final, the pick of which came in a 4–1 decimation of a very good Yugoslavia team. He picked up the ball near the halfway line, and his coruscating surge and swerve through midfield was only an omen for the drive that he eventually delivered, a right-footed bullet of a strike from almost thirty yards.

Barnes also identified a less celebrated but no less crucial reason for the perennial success of players like Matthäus (if, indeed, there ever was a player quite like Matthäus). 'The immunity from boredom is an aspect of sporting greatness', he wrote. 'Perhaps this quality is better understood as the ability to devote life and heart and mind and soul to a single thing.'

The English game in particular has always set great stall by this quality: another sense in which – much more than it would like – it resembles the German game. That doggedness of spirit was embodied most famously by Terry Butcher in a 1989 World Cup qualifier against Sweden, a goalless game in which he finished with a bandage tied tightly around his head, his shirt and head-dressing both soaked with blood. Were Butcher a German, Lothar Matthäus would have been proud.

I asked Barnes about this need for endurance, of having to have spent a prolonged spell at the top before you could be considered great. He was more flexible on this point than I'd expected, and was willing to indulge the same idea of greatness that had presumably appealed to the Hall of Fame's selection panel when their thoughts had fallen on Paul Gascoigne. 'There is a kind of greatness in the player who has the perfect season, or even perhaps the perfect goal', he explained. 'You wouldn't necessarily say that [Ryan] Giggs was there to be talked about in terms of greatness, but on the other hand he created that great season of 1999 by that wonderful goal against Arsenal.'

I've paid homage to that Giggs moment already, so I won't do so again; there's something to be said, though, for those athletes who produce moments so stunning that they go beyond the mere business of winning at competitive sport. Barnes recalled that 'I was speaking to a skater who said, "I don't want people to say she's a great skater, because she can do a triple axle, there's not a jump she can't triple. I don't want to be a skater. I just want to go past skating and they look at me and they say, that's a champion."'

There seemed to be, broadly speaking, two types of great footballer. First, there was the player for whom sustained pre-eminence was a hallmark in itself: someone like, say Arsenal's Tony Adams, who, if football was a company, was one of its most faithful employees. (As, indeed, were the rest of Arsenal's famous defence of the early to mid-1990s – Bould, Dixon, Winterburn, Keown and Seaman who seemed to last forever, stern and imposing as the faces on Mount Roosevelt.) Second, there was the footballer whose play you fell in love with: who could belong to the first category too, as did Johann Cruyff, but was generally more of a chancer, more irresponsible.

Fortunately, I had e-mailed my survey to, amongst other distinguished recipients, some poets, who'd provided me with some fluent and florid comments on that second class of player, and which I've happily reproduced below. Before I show you those, though, I must say that I was surprised to receive any completed football questionnaires from poets. It's interesting: the average poet will gladly hold forth in metaphor or simile about any aspect of the working-class man and woman – the angry youth on the Hackney night bus, the single mum on the breadline – but to ask for their views on football is generally to bellow into an echo chamber.

Football's known as the Beautiful Game, but it hasn't generated a glut of beautiful poetry; and that's a little strange, since it's not as if football's unaware of its own sense of romance. For example, the former England manager Terry Venables once spoke of a Zidane performance that was so good that it could have been set to music; Real Madrid, in their dominance of the early years of the European Cup, came to be christened as The White Ballet. In fact, it's a ballet anecdote, related by the eminent German journalist Uli Hesse-Lichtenberger, which is a good metaphor for the sometimes uneasy relationship between art and sport. 'A quarter of a century ago', wrote Hesse-Lichtenberger, 'Rudolf Nureyev attempted to seduce Franz Beckenbauer on the back seat of a limousine that was crawling through the streets of New York City. The famous dancer let his hand casually drop onto the Kaiser's knee, and a panicking Beckenbauer, familiar with Nureyev's reputation when it came to romance, immediately reeled off a monologue about his family back home. Nureyev got the message and withdrew his hand. The lesson to be learned from this should have been all too obvious: ballet and football don't mix.'

Whilst Beckenbauer was reluctant to bridge that divide, James O'Nuanain was happy to offer another artist's perspective. He felt that 'a great footballer is an oily concept to grab hold of. A sportsperson who embraces more than the adoration of their own discipline's fans to become some sort of cultural icon needs very particular qualities.' Helpfully, he then went on to set out some of these. 'They should either embody the dysfunctional excellence of an automaton: Schumacher, Tiger Woods, Jonny Wilkinson, and David Beckham all spring to mind, or they should have the spirited effortlessness of the talented lucky wastrel done well. George Best and Ronnie O'Sullivan spring to mind as great examples of the latter, perhaps no coincidence that they're both Irish. To be great, one doesn't have to be loved, but to be loved, you have to be well-rounded.'

Pete Sampras fitted easily into the automaton bracket, and so, sadly, many people seemed to start loving him only when he showed signs of suffering. Their enduring image of him wasn't Sampras clutching one of his seven Wimbledon trophies but weeping at the Australian Open over the terminal illness of one of his closest friends, his coach Tim Gullikson. (Incidentally, that's the reason why Gascoigne took a short cut to our hearts with his tears upon being booked in the 1990 World Cup semi-final against West Germany.) O'Nuanain then completed his analysis with an apparent paean to Gascoigne's rise and decline. 'When transferring to a new team they should either score in their first post-transfer match clinching the game in the fourth minute of injury time or they should go goalless for a twelve-match run before finally gaining a hat-trick against derby rivals or Premiership holders. The tears can be rapturous or relief turned to rapture but there must be tears ... They either should be brought low by drink and drugs or should play on past their best and at increasingly less glamorous clubs eventually becoming a coach. Whether it's whiskey, or dedication, there must be spirit.'

I received quite a few e-mails like this; several fans liked the idea of living vicariously through footballers, revelling (at a safe distance) in their rock 'n' roll lifestyles. There's always something exciting about watching others get away with things that you yourself never could, which explains literature's idolisation of Lord Byron, the original rock 'n' roll poet. (Byron, described by one of his lovers as 'mad, bad and dangerous to know', could probably have taught Gazza a thing or two about a night on the town.)

Inua Ellams, the other poet from whom I heard, was a different story; his poems featured metaphors that took brilliant flight within the first two or three lines, and so I was guaranteed an entirely separate slant on this issue. For him, being a great player wasn't about how long you'd endured in the game; it was about whether people wanted to emulate you. Ellams wrote that 'as one who knows not much about football, I am not in the best place to comment. However, there is a thing common in those that achieved greatness: the ability for the individual to reach outside his/her field (pun intended), to make such an impact in work that the person becomes a landmark to it and beyond. How many kids have acted out the 'Hand of God'? How many have attempted George Weah's post-to-post goal [for AC Milan against Verona]? ... For me, the greatness of a footballer comes after the pitch is black, after the crowd is gone, when there is no action, save the memories, flashbacks of the game, and the inspiration to take to life as the player takes to play.'

When I'd first read this, I disagreed; I'd taken a scientific approach to my eleven criteria so far, and endurance was the one to which I wanted to stick most firmly. It wasn't good enough, I'd reasoned, to do what Gascoigne did: to explode onto our horizons then dash away with the urgency of a comet, leaving us with only a few romantic brush strokes to remember him by. But then I began to prefer the artistic view that Ellams had put forward. When any of us are dribbling about in the park, trying clumsily to recreate that Peter Beardsley soft-boot shuffle or that Glenn Hoddle sidestep, we're not thinking about how many trophies they won, about their ratio of goals to games, about how many caps they won for England. We're thinking instead about the beauty of what they did, and we're hoping that, despite our poor ball control and our aching joints, we'll find some of their beauty within our feet: if only for one moment of one kick-about, that years from now, no one but us will even remember.

So I agree with Ellams; to be great, in one sense, is little to do with endurance. Instead, you have to create scenes that will live with people, long after you've ceased to, and it can take as few as one or two brilliant seasons for you to do that. The length of a player's career at the top isn't what makes him great; it's only what ranks him above other great players in the hierarchy. By that reasoning, since there's the small matter between them of three World Cups and an ocean of fulfilled potential, Gascoigne can't claim to be better than Pelé; but he would certainly still be fit to sit at the same table.

Graft

Invisible is not sexy. To win the admiring glances of spectators, football-ers must generally do that which is out of the ordinary, rather than immerse themselves in the mire of midfield. However, those players who toil, mostly unseen, are the ones who tend to receive lasting affection. France's Eric Cantona, an eye-catching sort of player, once infamously dismissed his compatriot Didier Deschamps as a 'water-carrier', a mere packhorse. Yet during his career Deschamps – whose ports of call included Marseille, Juventus and his national side – seemed not so much to carry water as to walk on it. He won every major team honour at club and international level, a feat almost repeated by Claude Makalélé, who inherited his place in the France midfield. Both of them, notably, won more and had a more decisive influence at the highest level than Cantona ever did. Why, then, are they often viewed as secondary citizens in the football world?

The answer is that it's partly their own fault, since they don't advertise themselves as well as they might. The grafter's ego – or, more to the point, his apparent lack of it – is essential if he wishes to play a sacrificial role for his team, which is why so often he ends up in defensive midfield. It's here that the game's finest grafters typically feature as the lesser light in a famous double act. When Andrea Pirlo plotted Italy's way to their 2006 World Cup triumph, he had Gennaro Gattuso bristling and bus-tling beside him. Juan Sebastian Verón, in his dominant days at Lazio, was minded by Matias Almeyda; Barça's Ronaldinho, as he set La Liga alight in his first season, was given his freedom to play by the quietly effervescent Xavi. Roy Keane, in his self-titled autobiography, speaks of his early rejection by a series of Football League clubs. In the process, he explains the grafter's predicament:

Looking back ... I understand what it was ... that the keen-eyed scouts didn't see. Brilliance. I was an all-rounder, I thought of myself as a team player. Although I could dominate midfield, I didn't go on mazy runs, beating man after man, or carving defences apart with forty-yard passes. I read the game, intercepted passes, cut off opposing players, passed the ball simply myself. I worked box to box, unceasingly, defending as well as I attacked. For every stunning goal I scored, and there were a few, there were a hundred little things, offensive and defensive, that went unnoticed. I worked for every second of a game with complete determination and absolute concentration. The determination was obvious, my trademark. The concentration was invisible.

Peter Shilton once said that there were some matches where, even though he hadn't had to make a single save, he'd been concentrating so hard that at the final whistle he'd leave the pitch drenched in sweat. Shilton's observation wasn't intended as a plea for pity, and nor were Keane's remarks about his failure to be noticed by the scouts. However, they're a salutary reminder that individual accolades rarely fall upon their sort. Indeed, a defensive midfielder has never won the *Ballon D'Or* for being Europe's best footballer, nor the FIFA World Player of the Year award. The closest anyone's ever come in that regard is Matthias Sammer, the German sweeper whose style and playing career at times resembled a homage to Franz Beckenbauer. Patrick Vieira, in his prime, never even finished in the top three nominations for either prize; tellingly, the same fate has befallen Raúl, arguably the most successful and probably the most hard-working striker of the modern era. This may be because video highlights of the prodigious work done with and without the ball by Vieira and Raúl – the reason why their teammates appreciate them so much – simply don't look as spectacular as those of other more flamboyant contenders. It's easy for the aesthete to salivate over the back-heels of Totti; it's a little harder for him to get worked up about a series of firm and patient five-yard passes. And, as is the case with major individual honours, it's the aesthetes who choose the winners.

The grafter, however, wouldn't be too taken aback by missing out on these honours, focusing as he does on the team ethic. And it shouldn't be thought that, while it contains some prosaic element, the defensive midfielder's role is an entirely unglamorous one. To have a nickname in the world of sport suggests that your level of play has risen above the mundane, and it's notable that grafters have their fair share of these: Marcel Desailly was 'the rock'; Gilberto Silva, of Arsenal and Brazil, the 'invisible wall'. Clodoaldo, the grafter behind the finest attack of all, the Brazil team of 1970, played in a role called the *cabeça de alho* (the 'clove of garlic'). Demetrio Albertini, in AC Milan's early 1990s glory years, was known as 'the metronome' for the steady and compelling tempo that his passes brought to his team's play. Real Madrid's Fernando Redondo was referred to as 'the prince'; whilst his successor in that shirt, Claude Makalélé, was described less elegantly but no less affectionately by the Chelsea coach Claudio Ranieri as 'the battery in my watch'.

There were yet more celebrated figures than Ranieri who came forward to sing Makalélé's praises, none less so than his erstwhile captain at Real Madrid. 'I think Claude has this kind of gift', Fernando Hierro has commented, 'he's been the best player in the team for years but people just don't notice him, don't notice what he does. But you ask anyone at Real Madrid during the years we were talking about and they will tell you he was the best player at Real. We all knew, the players all knew he was the most important. He was the base, the key... We knew he was the one player we could never do without.'

Steve McManaman agreed with this assessment. 'Makalélé, his first year in England, people thought he was useless, that he didn't do anything', he told me. 'But then people saw that [him being there] coincides with Frank [Lampard] scoring a thousand goals every season, because he had some bloke there just cleaning everything up for him... It was the same at Madrid. Nobody bothered about him, and then there was a big furore when he left. The people above couldn't see it, but the players really appreciated him. Since then they've gone out to buy five Makalélés and still haven't got a Makalélé ... they've tried everyone in that position, but they can't do it.'

Given this lack of appreciation for his talents, it's just as well that Makalélé had a healthy quotient of self-belief. *The Guardian*'s Sid Lowe asked him who he thought was the best player in the world, and – laughing, but probably serious – he replied: 'Makalélé. Ha, ha, ha, ha! Of course. Ha, ha, ha! Well, you've got to sell yourself, haven't you? Why am I the best in the world? Because I just am, that's all, heh, heh. No, I'm joking ... but you do have to believe in yourself, to sell yourself. There are too many great players to choose the very best in the world. So, it's me, then.'

The irony is that Real Madrid had once known all about the gently insistent grace that's found in uncomplicated football. Jorge Valdano, their sporting director, commented of the play of Fernando Redondo that 'there is music that takes time to relish. We listen to it without enthusiasm until one day we realise we've acquired the taste. With some players, the same thing happens – we resist them for a while and suddenly their most vehement critics discover a talent that had been seemingly very hidden.' It takes a strong ego, and no little humility, to contribute as much as did Redondo whilst remaining largely without recognition. But modesty was Redondo's legacy. When the Argentine was transferred from Madrid to Milan – sparking huge protest among fans who'd long since recognised his grace – he suffered a knee injury almost immediately. Barely playing in two years, he waived his claim to his salary, feeling that he hadn't earned it and so couldn't accept it in good conscience.

Redondo's understated style made him what Ron Atkinson – in one of his more lucid moments – called a 'continuity player' and what Phil Ball described to me as a *jugador vertical*. Atkinson was speaking of a footballer who manages to maintain the flow of the ball about the pitch, and Ball translated the word '*vertical*' as just that; as someone 'whose tendency is not to get the ball and pass it square, the general orientation of whose play is to get forward'. The Spanish league, with its style of fluid possession football, produces new models of the *jugador vertical* in abundance, the most recent and impressive incarnations of which are Barcelona's Xavi Hernandez and Andrés Iniesta. Clearly taken both by their endeavour and their deference, Ball has written that 'this is the beauty of Iniesta. Whilst all around him is fireworks, he just gets on with lighting the fuse. You don't actually notice him half the time. He hangs around in a vaguely forward position in midfield, always supporting the player with the ball, always available. He often just moves the ball on, like Xavi, ensuring that possession is retained.'

Grafters are the single mums of football: largely unheralded, they perform ceaseless, countless acts of silent heroism, taking a humble pleasure in each small task. The Russian Valery Karpin was perhaps the most diligent of mothers in this sense; John Toshack, his coach at Real Sociedad, said less than memorably of him that 'the great thing about Karpin is that he knows when to receive the ball and he knows when to pass it.' Bland as that may seem – bland as that is – it underpins the successful pass-and-move philosophy of the great Liverpool and Nottingham Forest teams of the late 1970s and early 1980s. To my mind, it also summed up the playing style of the midfielder Frank Rijkaard, the least celebrated of the three Dutchmen at AC Milan in the mid-Eighties. He was more effective than Ruud Gullit, almost to the level of van Basten; he grafted for them, he was, like Claude Makalélé, the base for their success. And so, growing up, I had always held out Frank Rijkaard as the embodiment of graft, but Simon Kuper told me otherwise:

> He wasn't a grafter. In fact, in his early years, the criticism was when he was at Ajax, they lost a European game against Bohemians Prague. And the coach said, 'you won't win the war with boys like Rijkaard' … it was a deadly thing to say about a 21-year-old kid. Ajax tried to sell Rijkaard to Groningen, a Dutch club, but they'd not have him.

According to Kuper, Rijkaard, whilst being the 'most impressive man I've met in football – the most intelligent, sophisticated, funny, psychologically astute; a truly A-1 human being – was seen as a pretty but lazy player', and he'd had to teach himself a work ethic. Of course, Rijkaard soon did that, proving pivotal to AC Milan's domestic and Continental triumphs, and even scoring the winning goal in the 1990 European Cup final against Sven-Goran Eriksson's Benfica.

But it's another, far earlier Continental triumph that shows best the value of graft. In 1967 Celtic, in the European Cup final, were faced by Internazionale and Helenio Herrera's *catenaccio* system. *Catenaccio* means padlock, which almost says it all: a form of football so defensive that it's excruciating on the eye, where the sweeper provides an additional line of security behind a deep-lying back four.

That day in Lisbon's Estádio Nacional, this method almost worked for Internazionale, their defence commanded by Italy mainstays Tarcisio Burgnich and Giacinto Facchetti. Much is often said of the need to 'break a team down', but the Italians weren't so much a team as an edifice. The inventor Thomas Edison told us that genius was one per cent inspiration, and ninety-nine per cent perspiration; Celtic's perspiration was more than evident in this encounter, and it's only numbers that can tell us the full story.

Internazionale, winners of this trophy twice in the previous three years, won no corners during the match; Celtic won ten. Internazionale mounted five attacks in ninety minutes; Celtic mounted forty-two. Even then, the decisive strike came only seven minutes from the end of the match, Stevie Chalmers deflecting home a low drive from Bobby Murdoch to give Celtic the victory. If this was a war of brilliant attrition from the Scots, then its most willing foot soldier was a creative player, that class of character most often maligned for its laziness; this was Jimmy Johnstone, whom his captain and centre-half Billy McNeill later said had beaten the Italians on his own. Kenny Dalglish, a Celtic man himself, once gave a glowing assessment of the career of John Barnes, but his words could also have doubled as praise for Johnstone's performance. 'Apart from being brilliant technically', said Dalglish, 'he also put in some shift... As well as scoring a few goals, he made a lot of goals, but he never ever shirked his share of work either on the pitch.'

Dalglish paid tribute to Barnes, but it was the Scotsman's predecessor at Anfield who was the blueprint for the diligent forward. Vic Wakeling reminded me of as much. 'Kevin Keegan – and I think he'll say this if you speak to him – was never what you might call the most naturally gifted player, but Kevin Keegan worked at his game', he said. 'From his very early days at Scunthorpe, he worked at his game, and he ended up being European Footballer of the Year twice. Outstanding. And he will tell you that in terms of basic skill, he was short of what the likes of George Best had … but he made the most of it. I think in this day and age, even now, that's what you need.'

David Ossack, a respondent to my survey, thought that whilst graft was needed, I'd overlooked a vital and related attribute: that of fitness. As he explained, 'Stamina should be included. There are many great Sunday-league players who simply don't have the fitness and never have to compete at a high level. Footballers are athletes and this is not reflected in your criteria.'

Ossack's point flagged up what was perhaps a changing emphasis in the football world. His comment – that 'footballers are athletes' – wouldn't raise an eyebrow now, but there was a time when, certainly in England, the two professions were not synonymous. On the Continent, Arrigo Sacchi's AC Milan, on their way to two European Cups in the early 1990s, played a pressing game that was regarded as revolutionary: the idea being that the opposition should be harried out of possession all over the pitch. Twenty years earlier, Don Revie's Leeds United had taken a similar approach, using sheer stamina; but this is a thing of the past. True, the dietary misadventures of many British stars were a shock to the first foreign coaches who came to the Premiership, but fitness is now near the very top of football's agenda. At the beginning of July 2006 Simon Kuper, in a dryly disdainful article in *The Financial Times*, went so far as to suggest that the German national team's US-style training techniques might be 'the only footballing innovation of this World Cup'. He continued:

American sports probably have the best physical methods, but hardly anyone in soccer knows that. The average European football coach is a middle-aged bloke who has never physically been inside a university. If he wants players to run faster, he gives them the exercises he did as a player 25 years before. But an American sports coach – even at a high school – chairs a battery of specialists. If he wants his players to run faster, a university department provides the latest research on sprint training.

Jürgen Klinsmann, the German coach for that tournament, adopted the American approach and thus remained ahead of the game, his unfancied side reaching the semi-finals and losing very narrowly to Italy, who of course went on to win. On the subject of major tournaments, it's notable that several teams outside the pantheon of football's superpowers are now advancing further than might be expected; most spectacular were the cases of South Korea, who reached the World Cup semi-finals in 2002, and Greece, who won the 2004 European Championship. There were several factors behind the success of the South Koreans and the Greeks, not least, in the Koreans' case, their home advantage, and, more importantly, excellent coaching by Guus Hiddink and Otto Rehhagel respectively. But there's also the sense that the World Cup and the European Championship have more of an element of the fitness lottery about them than they did previously; that is to say, that the teams whose players enjoy the most rest prior to the tournament have the best chance of winning.

This is a banal observation, but it wasn't so obvious to the bookmakers, some of whom quoted Greece – the team whose players were among the fittest, and certainly the most relaxed – at odds of 100–1 to win Euro 2004. Theirs was an instructive case: several of their footballers were mainstays for lesser teams, or were fringe players for top sides; for example, Stelios Giannakopoulos was an underrated playmaker at Bolton, and their defenders Takis Fyssas and Traianos Dellas were respected, if underused, at Benfica and Roma. The Greeks were therefore enjoying the benefits of first-class training facilities at their clubs, whilst not being involved in the taxing later stages of international club competition. It's a welcome sight to see the unfancied teams breaking rank from the game's traditional hierarchy, but it's a joy tempered by the fact that it's fitness regimes, and not high technique, that have become the democratising force in world football.

There's another essential characteristic that's similar to graft, which is the ability and willingness to perform for your team all over the pitch. It was Chris Bushell who e-mailed me to suggest that I'd omitted this element from my survey. 'Utility', he wrote; '[Alfredo] di Stefano was a centre-forward but he could also play in defence and midfield.' I considered this an aspect of graft rather than a separate element, but I agreed with Bushell's suggestion. So did Steve McManaman: 'You have to adapt', he said. 'You have to be able to play in three, four, five positions these days, otherwise you won't make it.' We noted that, for Real Madrid, McManaman had played at right-wing, left-wing, right-back and in central midfield, and he identified another recent example of such versatility. 'You can see Ryan Giggs now. He can play centre-forward, he can play left-wing, he's played centre midfield, he could play right-wing without a doubt, he could play left-back if he wanted to. And you have to be able to do that.'

The role of the utility player is one that's frequently stigmatised in football, despite having been recently filled by stars such as the Bosnian Hasan Salihamidžić, Spain's Luis Enrique, and Italy's Gianluca Zambrotta. In England it's considered that they're not masters of any one trade, but jacks of all, and that a footballer of real repute should have one specialist position that he can call his own: hence the umbrage taken by most sections of the media when Steven Gerrard was played on the right side of Liverpool's midfield for several games at the beginning of the 2007–8 season. The argument in that instance was more that Gerrard was wasted on the flank, but Rafael Benitez was entitled to expect one of his best players to be one of his most versatile. Chelsea's Michael Essien, after all, was producing exceptional performances each week during the same period, despite being deployed at right-back, right-wing, centre-midfield and centre-back.

Of course, there are earlier examples of more distinguished players flourishing in positions that wouldn't have been their first choice. Ruud Gullit arrived at AC Milan in 1988 as a goalscoring midfielder of the highest rank, but prior to that he'd played as a sweeper at Feyenoord. (Incidentally, how defensive he truly was in that role is open to question. In 1984, as Feyenoord won the *Eredivisie*, the Dutch first division title, he'd helped himself to 24 goals, the world record for an occupant of that position.) Lothar Matthäus, the 1990 World Cup-winning captain of West Germany, as it then was, also followed the format of Gullit's career, albeit in reverse order to the charismatic Dutchman; he'd started out as an attacking midfielder, before returning to the more tranquil pasture of sweeper in his later thirties. Aside from their fine fitness levels, Gullit and Matthäus were also able to adapt as well as they did due to their reading of the game, which few could match. In that sense, they were as close to the ideal of the total footballer as anyone's ever been, and in Michael Essien, we've seen the renewed celebration of that ideal.

It shouldn't be thought, though, that British players haven't followed this fashion. In fact, in the form of England's Duncan Edwards and Wales' John Charles, the UK can boast two of the earliest and most enduring examples of the total footballer. When I'd first explained the concept of this book to him, Simon Barnes had reminded me (or, given the complexity of my task, cautioned me) that there were many different forms of greatness, and it seems that the greatness of Edwards was based upon his commitment. The Manchester United footballer, who'd perished in the Munich air disaster of 6 February 1958, was, by all accounts, the consummate professional wherever he was asked to play; he operated at left-half, although his power, touch and mobility suggest that he'd have been happy anywhere. Sadly, there's little footage available from Edwards' era, so it's hard to see just how good he was: the best that I could find was a tantalising video clip, less than two minutes long, of a player tearing through tackles, sweeping a ball forty elegant yards out to the left wing, a source of ceaseless energy. Sir Bobby Charlton, a man not noted for his hyperbole, thought Edwards the greatest player he'd ever seen:

> For Duncan, there was no such thing as an unimportant match. He gave one hundred per cent in the lot. I think that supplies the key

to his genius... There were probably small-time army games when he thought he'd have a quiet cruise through – just keep out of trouble and not overtire himself for the next international or league match. But, once the game started, everything else went out of his mind. He ran and tackled and surged through as if his reputation depended on it. Whether it was Wembley or on a bumpy pitch behind the barracks, he became immersed in it.

That indomitable will was in evidence during the most tragic of occasions; after the crash, during which seven teammates and fifteen other people had died, Edwards survived for fifteen days before succumbing to multiple and severe internal injuries. The fighting spirit of Edwards is alive and well in today's Premiership, though this stems more from necessity than from any desire to carry a torch for the legendary Mancunian. According to ProZone, who provide a detailed statistical breakdown of player performance over the course of a match, graft is a fact of life. As revealed by their statistics for the 2005–6 season, players are running if not further, then faster, than ever. As Jonathan Northcroft reported in *The Sunday Times* in May 2006:

The average distance covered by players in matches has changed little in the last four seasons but the amount done at top speed has almost doubled. What ProZone class as 'high-intensity activities' – runs made by players at three-quarters of sprint pace or faster – have increased from 627 per team per match in 2002–3 to 1,209 in 2005–6, and the ground covered by players while sprinting has increased by 40% over four years. A sprint is classed as a run made at quicker than seven metres per second, equivalent to running 100m in a sharp 14 seconds.

Men of Edwards' mentality, if not his proficiency, are now par for the course. When discussing Gerrard's capacity for hard work with Bolo Zenden, I'd received a mildly-puzzled raised eyebrow from the Dutch-man, as if confirming, as Northcroft had noted elsewhere in his article, that the Liverpool number-eight was not exceptional among his peers in terms of stamina.

The highest accolade that any grafter can gain is to be viewed as a true professional. Indeed it's 'the good pro' who received Eamon Dunphy's dedication at the start of *Only a Game?*, the Ireland midfielder's seminal fly-on-the-wall account of his troubled year at Second Division side Millwall in the early 1970s. Those who see a place for integrity and sportsmanship in the soul of the great player would be reassured by Dunphy's lengthy praise of 'the good pro', which is as poetic and passionate as any piece of sporting prose that you'll see. In his introduction to the 1986 edition of the book, he writes:

> I believe the good pro was the true hero of professional sport ... The good pro is a trier – not one of those despised young automatons that pass for midfield players these days, all sweat and crunching tackles, but a much nobler embodiment of sporting virtue. The good pro accepts responsibility – both his and, when the going gets tough, yours ... He is woven into the fabric of every good side and every great side too ... In attack or defence, at home or away, in January mud, April wind or August sunshine, every game is a test and there are so many ways to cheat, to walk away from your responsibility to the team. The good pro never does. He is sometimes knackered, often in despair, but never out of the ball game, never on the missing list ... He is the footballer's footballer.

That's a heart-warming profile, smugly Corinthian in tone, but we can't get carried away with it; the primary aim in professional sport is victory, and that aim often involves methods that have a certain moral ambivalence. That's why 'graft' is an odd but fitting word in this context, in that it has two meanings: it can simply mean 'hard work', but it also has a more sinister edge; it can also mean to scam your way to the top, to get ahead without scruple. This isn't the interpretation that most people probably had in mind when answering my survey, but maybe that trace of gamesmanship lurks beneath the surface of most footballers. It's not that athletes necessarily set out to defeat their opponents by any necessary means; it's just that sport at the highest level is a matter of infinitesimal margins, and if there's a fair or foul way to seize that advantage, the temptation to take it will always be there.

Any Given Sunday, a film about American football, is remarkable only for a short speech about graft. Delivered by Al Pacino, it's an address so inspirational that by itself it justifies the price of the video rental: Pacino, as the coach of the fictional Dallas Knights, gives a rousing send-off to his team before they run up the tunnel, and he tells them about those margins I mentioned in the previous paragraph, so small that they measure only inches. Pacino, with that controlled and slowly rising roar that made him, tells his team:

> On this team, we fight for that inch; on this team, we tear ourselves, and everyone around us, to pieces for that inch; we claw with our finger nails for that inch; 'cause we know, when we add up all those inches, that's going to make the fucking difference between winning and losing; between living and dying... I'll tell you this: in any fight, it is the guy who is willing to die who is going to win that inch; and I know, if I am going to have any life anymore it is because I am still willing to fight and die for that inch, because that is what living is.

This speech, complete with the whole Hollywood backdrop of softly-plucked yet stirring strings, is the one passage of film over which it's socially permissible for the male sports fan to burst into tears. What's more, it tells us about the amoral element of winning: because in that moment, when you're going for that inch, then things like valour can all too easily fall away, and all of Dunphy's romantic notions of 'the good pro' with them. Which brings us to the man who most memorably stole that extra inch, in that World Cup quarter-final as the ball looped, drifted just beyond his reach, towards the goalkeeper's outstretched fist; that's when Diego Maradona stretched out his own arm and tipped the ball over Peter Shilton, for what was football's – and perhaps, sport's – defining moment of graft.

It's not necessarily being argued here that every great player must cheat if winning requires it. But he'll have to do things that, in the cold light of day, might raise the eyebrows of the ethical guardian: he'll have to leave a leg trailing in that tackle for that penalty, or pull that shirt when the referee's distracted; and if he's a member of the opposition we'll call him a cheat, and if he's one of our own we'll say that he's been 'cute', that he's 'used his experience'. (After all, that's how we England fans rationalised Michael Owen's penalty-box plummet against Argentina in the 1998 World Cup.)

When England play Argentina, graft will always play a part, one way or another. Historically, there has always been so little between the two teams that the victor is always the side who, frankly, expresses the more naked will. Maradona knew this in 1986, and so did Gary Lineker, who'd been on the losing side that day. Lineker cornered him several years later in Argentina for an interview, and asked him about the Hand of God; which you could look at either as a symbol of Diego's desperation after the previous two World Cups hadn't gone his way, or as plain, old-fashioned cheating. Maradona was oddly uneasy as he was quizzed, suggesting that he wasn't as proud of the incident as he'd claimed in his autobiography, where he'd written of having 'pickpocketed' the English. Watching Gary Lineker smile, as he gently questioned Maradona was as morbidly engrossing as watching the killer clown grinning at the child in a horror movie. When pressed on the issue of his graft, El Diego answered haltingly:

> I don't think it's cheating. It's cunning, it's cheekiness, it can be handling the ball, or … or … no, no, no, it's not cheating. I don't … I don't think it's cheating. I believe it's, ah, a craftiness. Maybe we have a lot more of it in South America than in Europe, but, ah, it's not cheating.

Toughness

The hard man is a feature of any successful football team: its guardian, its cornerstone, and its dark heart. As a result, any player who wishes to earn his spurs at the highest level must either contend with one of them, or be one of them. The hard men are the anvils upon which the reputations of many opponents are beaten or broken altogether. Diego Maradona fell foul of Andoni Goikoetxea, the 'Butcher of Bilbao', when he faced him in Spain in the early 1980s; however, Maradona returned to make an even greater mark on the game than this 'Butcher' had made on his shins. Remarkably, though, there's no similarly camp nickname recorded for Paolo Montero, of Uruguay and Juventus, even though he was sent off more times than anyone else in the history of Italy's Serie A. Montero was proud of his status as aggressor-in-chief. Although he described himself away from the game as 'a romantic, a shy one', he became, each time he took the field, the walking embodiment of horror itself. He understood that to be the tough guy is as much a role play as it is a responsibility.

To date, there's been no shortage of actors to play him. Vinnie Jones, before he departed to Hollywood, was one such. For example, there's the legendary incident where he grabbed and crushed Paul Gascoigne's testicles in a First Division match. Only slightly less well known is that he terrified one of the modern game's hard men, who was none other than Arsenal's Patrick Vieira. As Vieira recounts in his autobiography:

> Since I have been in England, only one player has frightened me: Vinnie Jones, who I played against when he was at Aston Villa. It was enough for me just to look at him to feel afraid. He didn't speak. But there was pure nastiness in his eyes and in the vibes that he gave

off. You could feel that you were not safe when you were playing against him.

Vieira wasn't entirely wrong: in 1998, Jones was convicted for assault against his neighbour, occasioning actual bodily harm. However, his confession of fear could be seen to have marked a disturbing trend for some in the game of football, and in the English game above all. If the hard men were getting scared in the heat of battle, then what next? This concern that football was 'going soft' was expressed nowhere more forcefully than in Hunter Davies' introduction to the 2001 edition of *The Glory Game*, as he discussed the training methods of Eddie Baily, a member of the coaching staff at Tottenham Hotspur in the early 1970s. Davies wrote that 'the sort of Second World War language and metaphors with which Eddie Baily used to exhort his troops, urging them over the top, were still typical of the times. Both he and Bill had been in the army, had seen men act like men, not these long-haired fairies.'

Many other football fans, players and writers have lamented the passing of these good old days, where tackles were hard but fair, and where they were unfair, it didn't matter quite so much. To hear Davies tell it, football's undergone a steady evolution from tough but fair play to a somewhat feminised edition of its former self, where diving is increasingly commonplace. That's an argument with much force, but it meets opposition – somewhat surprisingly – from the shy and romantic Paolo Montero, who believed that 'football is all about cunning'. He expanded on this theme, stating that 'I would never criticise a forward who simulates. It has been like that since football was invented. Once upon a time, without television, these things were worse and there weren't all the debates that there are now … it is different on the field because you need to win by whatever means, even though being cunning is neither dishonest nor unfair.'

This disagreement between Davies and Montero shows that, in football, it's fine to pretend to be the aggressor, but not to pretend to be the victim. These schools of thought could be broadly, crudely, rendered as English and South American, and Martin Amis has provided an interesting perspective on the latter. In his review of *El Diego*, Diego Maradona's autobiography, he comments that 'for the Argie macho (or so this slanderous generalisation runs) foul means are incomparably more satisfying than fair … There is in this culture a humiliation, an abjectness, in always playing by the rules.'

Amis's piece shows the slightly rose-tinted view that English football has of itself: as a game whose Corinthian values have been steadily eroded by the arrival of foreigners, as if diving to win penalties were a skill simply imported to the UK along with textiles and demerara sugar. Norman Hunter, an abrasive defender at Leeds United during their 1970s heyday, puts this fiction to rest in his autobiography, *Biting Talk*. He noted that 'people write and talk about present-day players diving in a bid to win a penalty but Franny [England international Francis Lee] and Rodney Marsh were absolutely brilliant at it back in my day. They used to run straight at you with the ball, knock it past you and then go down.' Once himself referred to as football's hardest man, Hunter has helpfully provided as good a working definition of 'the hard man' as any. 'There are two ways of looking at being a hard man', he wrote. 'I was aware of what was going on in a game and saw danger coming. I still went into the tackle but I used to protect myself accordingly. The real hard men were those who went into challenges without even sensing danger or caring how they might end up. They were truly fearless.'

Hunter, for his own part, considered himself 'a bit of a softy, really', but it's difficult to reconcile that with his nickname, 'Bites Yer Legs'. Though Hunter's wife didn't really care for this violent moniker, there have been others in the football world who would have relished it. But, beneath the hard man's bravado, an insecurity can be detected. This is implicit in a short but telling scene in Simon Kuper's vivid football history, *Ajax, The Dutch, The War*, when Puck van Heel, the Feyenoord captain, stands on the foot of Meijer Stad as they await a corner. Stad recalls to Kuper that he shouted at van Heel, 'Hey, what are you doing?' and van Heel replied, 'Boy, when you're as old as I am, you'll do that to another.' Whilst van Heel's deficiency here was his age, the hard man's weakness is often his inferior technique, which is why he often finds himself playing the role of the grafter. Several of the defensive stars whom we may now revere – such as Sol Campbell, or Ashley Cole – began their careers as forwards or playmakers, moving to positions further downfield as they joined teams where players had far greater vision than themselves. In a sport of such flammable egos, it's a humbling demotion for these players to have undergone: to go from being the architect of your team's attacks, to the destroyer of the opposition's.

But some players remain refreshingly free of vanity. Stuart Pearce, or 'Psycho' to his victims, made no pretensions to delicacy on the ball, though like many powerful full backs of his era, his touch was far better than advertised. Pearce, capped seventy-eight times for England, built a fine career upon calculated intimidation: he knew which buttons to push, and when to push them. As he commented in his autobiography, 'Football revolves around little battles. You know you can scare the life out of some and others aren't troubled and you have to handle them differently.' And that's where the sophistication – if that's the right word – is to be found in the tough guy's role. Any meandering goon can use his studs to carve sculptures in his foes, but it takes finesse, carefully crafted aggression, to get away with it.

The level of finesse needed has risen with the passing of time. As mentioned earlier, some gruffly attribute this to the fact that football is losing its physical edge; but the answer's more mundane than that, and was supplied by Montero earlier. Simply put, the advent of technology has created a greater culture of scrutiny in football than ever before. With disciplinary committees keen to impose severe punishments on the basis of video evidence, the modern hard man must be ever more diligent when going about his destructive business. Moreover, the slow-motion savagery of a television replay takes the original foul out of its heated context. With each shuddering frame watched again and again, that defender's raised arm starts to look more and more like a smartly-aimed elbow, and its intent upon contact looks less reckless and increasingly murderous. Hard men, therefore, are being forced to work within ever narrower parameters, but that's no bad thing.

This was shown most plainly by the Portuguese midfielder Mário

Coluna, who like most self-respecting hatchet men had his own nick-name – the ominous *O Monstro Sagrado*, or 'the sacred monster'. In the 1966 World Cup, his side met Pelé, and as captain he made it his duty to man-mark him; there was nothing novel in this mission. However, that match was conspicious both for the venom with which he pursued his aim, and for the shamelessness with which it was done. He caught Pelé once, and then, almost as soon as Pelé had prised himself from the turf, he caught him again. It was a brutal one-two, a pair of challenges where he used his sturdy legs like pincers around Pelé's ankles. Most notable here was the casual fashion in which Coluna jogged away, secure in the knowledge that football was a man's game, that his actions would go unpunished, and thus tacitly approved.

A man's game, then, but what kind of man? There was no great skill, of thought or execution, in such a thuggish approach. There was even something cowardly on Coluna's part, in that he feared even to tackle an equal share of man and ball, concerned that he'd end up with neither. Unlike the superb stalemate that Bobby Moore and Pelé would contest at the World Cup in Mexico four years later, where striker and centre half would fight each other to a thunderous standstill, Coluna couldn't claim to have won a hard-fought match-up against the Brazilian. Though his twin assault put Pelé out of the tournament, his tactics were the first to concede that he couldn't have beaten him fair and square.

This is, then, what made Fernando Hierro so special: he was equally at home playing fair or dirty. Vic Wakeling warned me to be cautious of 'the perception that old-fashioned defenders were big, rough, tough-tackling guys who just thumped in, and won the ball, and away it went', and Hierro could easily have been his case in point. A defender and midfielder with Real Madrid for fourteen years, and Spain for eighty-nine internationals, he made no concessions to attackers. Technically, he was almost matchless in his role – there can have been few centre backs, or indeed central midfielders, so elegant in possession of the ball. He scored more than a goal every five games in the colours of Real Madrid, in almost six hundred appearances. At the same time, he shared the precise ruthlessness of Montero, to the extent that he was the most carded player in the history of the Spanish league by the time of his retirement. He has thus explained his dominance of several areas of the field at once: 'I'm a defender by definition, but not at heart. I've always maintained that I'm a defender with the heart and soul of a forward… honestly, deep down, I know I wasn't born to defend.'

What Hierro was born to do was to assert his team's superiority throughout the game, by force of will as much as anything else. There was a moment in a La Liga game against Real Zaragoza when Juanele darted impertinently across the face of the Madrid midfield, tapping the ball just beyond the reach of yearning defenders, in a dribble that was meant to mock and embarrass. Seeing two teammates stagger in Juanele's wake, Hierro stepped forward and caught Juanele late on the edge of the centre circle, a carefully mistimed scythe of which Coluna would have been proud.

Teammates invest much in players like Hierro; so artful is their aggression that they are each regarded as the talisman of their side, its true axis more surely than any mere playmaker could be. In the postscript to Patrick Vieira's autobiography, France's Lilian Thuram wrote in similarly approving prose of his international colleague:

It's a bit like when a plane hits turbulence: the passengers will look at the air hostesses to read their body language. If they look calm and authoritative, the passengers will take their calm from that and be reassured. That's what it's like playing in Patrick's teams. He'll always be there, fearless, never giving up.

By that token, Real Madrid's failure to secure the signature of Patrick Vieira in 2004 can be seen as an enormous transfer market mistake. Hierro, by then in his late thirties, had been dispatched with disrespectful speed; as Robbie Fowler commented wryly in his autobiography, 'believe me, there's no sentiment in football'. At that time, Real were thus looking for not just a marshal for their midfield and defence, but for an heir to Hierro's throne. At the time of the intended purchase, there was more at stake than Madrid ever realised.

Football teams are constantly trying to build empires, and Real Madrid are perhaps the originators of this trend; if not, they're certainly its finest proponents. They've enjoyed two golden ages in European football, the first occurring when they won six European Cups in the 1950s and 1960s, including five in a row, and the second between 1998 and 2002, when they won the European Cup (by now renamed as the Champions League) a further three times. By 2004, they were at a curious crossroads. They had assembled, by general consensus, the greatest attacking talent that the game had ever seen. Among their ranks were Ronaldo, Luis Figo, and Zinedine Zidane, each of whom had been the FIFA World Player of the Year; David Beckham, who'd finished within the top three for this award; Roberto Carlos, a left back of relentless energy; and Raúl, arguably the most effective of them all. But they'd no hard man. Negotiations with Vieira failed at the very last minute, but a more concerted campaign by Madrid might have got them their man: and if they had, they could have become unstoppable. And how they needed Vieira. His resolve could have provided the platform for Madrid's third golden age in Europe; football teams build their success upon momentum, and his arrival could have halted in its tracks the ascent of Ronaldinho and Barcelona. As it was, though, Vieira spent a final ineffectual, disaffected season at Arsenal, before being transferred to Juventus. Real Madrid, meanwhile, failed in both La Liga and Europe.

If this episode showed anything above all, it's that the hard man's the hardest member of a team to replace. The Liverpool team of the early 1990s lacked someone who could harness the youthful verve of Robbie Fowler, Steve McManaman and other assorted stars, which is why – like Real a decade later – they never built the momentum that would see them entirely justify the high regard in which they were held. The irony was that this Liverpool side was managed by an ex-player who, had he recruited a midfielder in his own image, would have led them to extraordinary heights. Scotland's Graeme Souness, winner of five championships and three European Cups in the early 1980s, was appointed in order to restore the Merseyside outfit to its rightful place atop the League hierarchy. The thinking was that his prowess as a footballer would naturally transfer to his prowess as a manager; yet, as Bryan Robson and Arsène Wenger have shown in different ways, there's not necessarily any correlation between the two.

This was a shame for Souness, whose struggles as Liverpool manager have threatened to overshadow his legacy there as a player. The Italians once described Zinedine Zidane as a 'four-wheel drive', a midfielder who'd mastered all of the arts of the game (even, presumably, the darker ones); and this phrase could equally have been applied to the Scotsman. Such was the fury with which he challenged for the ball, such was the tenderness with which he then treated it, that it was as if he were rescuing a kidnapped infant. In his day, the primary creative force would have come from elsewhere in the team; but, as Simon Kuper explained to me, the game was undergoing a subtle but marked transition:

The 2001 World Youth Cup final was Argentina–Ghana. Argentina were fabulous, and Saviola was man of the tournament, and they beat Ghana quite easily in the final. So Saviola was bought by Barcelona off the back of that tournament. And of course, now, nobody wants Saviola, he's a reserve, because he's that old-fashioned number ten. And the Ghana central midfielder that day was Michael Essien, who's now the most desirable central midfielder in the world, because he's the strong man in central midfield. So in 2001 the fashion was still for the Saviola type – it was thought that if you had a brilliant number ten, that was your most important player – whereas now coaches believe, like Mourinho, that your most important player is your hard man, who can also play football.

Meanwhile, Steve McManaman had perceived the same trend as had Kuper. As he told me: 'When Arsenal beat Liverpool 6–3 [in the 2006–7 Carling Cup quarter-final at Anfield] I was in the crowd, and the physical stature of these people ... they were like men and boys. I mean, Liverpool had a couple of big lads out there, but the Arsenal fellas were so big, strong and powerful, and you just thought to yourself, "bloody hell".'

Arsenal had been overwhelming that night, the first team to score six goals at Liverpool's ground since Sunderland in the 1929–30 season. The symbol of their remarkable power was the Brazilian Julio Baptista, more famously known as the 'Beast', who savaged the home side's defence for four goals that evening: a lightweight unit this was not. It's premature, then, to regard football as a game whose players are getting progressively less robust; you might say that this reflects the cyclical nature of the sport, alternating between phases of being slow and leisurely, and then fast and physical. It's difficult to anticipate how much more aggressive football will become in its present incarnation. It's fair to say, though, that it won't go as far as the previous extent described by the Association of Football Statisticians in its *History of Football*:

> The football field was the length of the town, the players might be as many as five hundred, the conflict continued all day long; vast numbers of windows and legs were broken, and there were even some deaths.

There's no getting away from the fact that the dressing room can be a uniquely vicious place. Upon his retirement from the game, Sunderland's Niall Quinn, renowned as one of football's nice guys, gave the entire proceeds of his testimonial – around a million pounds – to charity: a gesture for which he was rightly, and widely, applauded. Quinn saw his donation as a chance to put something back into the game, but he also saw it as an act of atonement for the occasions when, in the course of mocking a less talented or successful teammate, he may have taken the abuse too far. Robbie Fowler lifted the lid on this mentality when he remarked that 'if you are going to make it in football, then you've got to be able to take all the jokes and banter that go on in a world where most people are aggressive, competitive working-class lads with little or no education ... you have to be able to put up with so much shit because you want it so badly.'

As you read Fowler's frank social commentary, you can imagine him writing it with a gentle shrug of the shoulders: boys will be boys. This view would be supported by Martin Blake, a midfielder who was in

Manchester United's youth system alongside Ryan Giggs (who was then Ryan Wilson). Blake, a City trader who left United and then went on to Port Vale before leaving football altogether, was especially forthright when I asked him about the game's dressing room culture. 'It all kicks off … there's loads that goes on in football clubs', he said, before going on to describe a fairly bracing immersion technique:

> At Port Vale, whenever it was someone's birthday, they'd fill a bath with water and all the pros would put everything in it – shit, piss, liniment – and they'd dunk you in it three times. And they'd hurt you if you didn't do it, it'd be free-for-all battery … my initiation at Port Vale was getting my balls polished with boot polish and a wire brush.

To bathe in faeces and to have balls scoured: these experiences were enough to sour most people on the dream of becoming a professional footballer. Blake seemed quite happy to be out of it all, particularly Sir Alex Ferguson's quasi-corporate regime at Old Trafford. 'He was a hard, hard, hard bastard', he recalled. '[He and the coaching staff] were trying to be as nice as possible, but they were cut-throat.' Blake also served up an intriguing piece of information. Despite Ferguson's steely professionalism, it's widely acknowledged that he was on the brink of dismissal in 1990, and that he was only saved by Manchester United's FA Cup triumph that year. In fact, the turning point in Ferguson's career at the Theatre of Dreams is routinely traced back to a nervy 1–0 victory in the third round of that competition. But, contrary to popular perception, Blake pours scorn on the suggestion that Ferguson's job had ever been in doubt. 'He was nowhere near leaving', says Blake emphatically. 'Him and Archie Knox [his assistant] used to work till 10 p.m. each night, and Bobby Charlton used to come down to the Cliff [Manchester United's training ground] to watch the likes of Beckham and Scholes. And then Bobby Charlton would go back and talk to the directors and say, "don't you worry, just you wait till you see [the young players] we've got coming through."'

Blake's account of the hard edge to a professional's life was whole-heartedly confirmed by an ex-professional I spoke with, who'd played for three years at a leading northern Premiership club in the mid-1990s. He told me of a world where players were often so terrified of the pressure from the crowd that they'd feign injury, so that they could delay their return to action. This was also a world where, in his first training session, he was raked hard, high and late down the back of his calves, and told, 'welcome to professional football', and the worst players in training were forced to stand in corners and pelted with flying boots. Anecdotes such as these show the extensive vetting process and what it takes to get to the top, much of which the great players will have endured, if not initiated themselves.

Moreover, they give something of a lie to the common stereotype of the 'pampered footballer'; the stereotype may hold true for that handful who are eternally in the spotlight, but in many respects dressing rooms are the barracks of the sports world. There's nothing new in that, and it's not likely to change anytime soon: the law considers that there's no place for a softness of approach in environments that are overflowing with testosterone. As Lord Mustill commented in the House of Lords case of *R v Brown*:

> The law recognises that community life (and particularly male community life), such as exists in the school playground, in the barrack room and on the factory floor, may involve a mutual risk of deliberate physical contact in which a particular recipient may come off worst, and that the criminal law cannot be too tender about the susceptibilities of those involved.

Amid Martin Blake's bracing tales of 'male community life', there was one other comment – or rather, request – of his that was particularly memorable. Whilst discussing the unstoppable rise of Ryan Giggs through the youth ranks at Manchester United, he'd paused, and then asked: 'Have you ever heard of Raphael Burke?' I said no, I hadn't. 'You have to find Raphael Burke, you have to talk to him', insisted Blake. It turned out that Burke, a sensational forward, had been in the same year as Giggs at Manchester United, a year above the elite class of Beckham, Scholes, Butt and the Nevilles. 'He was the biggest thing in English football!' Bigger than Giggs, I wondered. Ryan Giggs, in his autobiography, was unequivocal. He'd described the fourteen-year-old Raphael Burke as 'the best player in the area at that age. I was an apprentice with him at United later, and I was surprised that he never made it. He was a right winger, one of those kids who is unbelievable at fourteen, but doesn't train on … I looked at players like Nicky Barmby and Raphael Burke, who were fantastic at that age, and thought I wasn't in the same class.'

This left me intrigued. How could so promising a talent have vanished without trace? As soon as I returned home I searched for Raphael Burke, and he was surprisingly easy to find. A quick internet search revealed that he was still involved in football, working for World Sports Ministries as a coach for children in the Bristol area. In my mind, more questions swiftly formed themselves. Had he turned his back on professional football to use his athletic gifts in aid of the Church? Had he encountered dressing room discrimination because of his faith? After all, Va'aiga Tuigamala, the legendary All Blacks winger, had once said that 'it is quite amazing how people do not bat an eyelid if you are into the new-age movement or Eastern religion, but if you say you are a born-again Christian, a follower of Jesus Christ, they freak out.'

But as I spoke to Burke over the telephone, it quickly became clear that religion hadn't played a part in his disappearance from the ranks at Manchester United. I'd expected him to be more rueful that it hadn't worked out for him there, but he was far from that; in fact, his enthusiasm was infectious, having swapped the passion of Old Trafford for that of Christ. 'Being a top footballer is not my priority', he said simply; 'being able to fund the kingdom of God is my priority.' Warm and engaging, he was very frank about what had led to his footballing demise. 'My coach said that I'm the biggest disappointment he's ever had … and it wasn't because I was a bad player, because Ryan Giggs said I was a brilliant player. The difference between a top player and a poor player isn't technical, it's mental.' When I outlined again the premise for the book that I was writing, to explore the eleven elements that I considered were present in all of the great footballers, he told me that I should rank one element above all others. 'Forget ability, forget quickness – it's about the mind. You can talk about quick feet, and the rest, but you can only do what your mind lets you do. That's it. Full stop, forget all the rest.'

Burke's career had preceded the era of sports psychologists, and so he'd faltered at the final, crucial hurdle: the mental one. 'To go and stand in front of eighty-thousand fans and an audience of two million is very different from doing it on the training ground', he explained, and applauded the attitude of one of English football's future greats. 'When Wayne Rooney puts the ball down on the penalty spot, in his head he's already celebrating, he's already seen the back of the papers, and he's seen his mates running over to celebrate with him. You've got to think like that… A top player makes the crowd work for him. When Rooney steps onto the pitch, he thinks, "They've come to see me, to see how good I am." A poor player works for the crowd. He thinks, "If I don't do it, make it happen, the crowd will get on my back."' He then finished with an appropriately Biblical flourish: 'That attitude brings him poverty on the pitch.'

When I mentioned Burke's comments to Hugh McIlvanney, he agreed, noting that the pressures of a big club affect 'even guys who've got a fair way along in the game. You know, there's a fellow who came down from Scotland to Liverpool – Paul McGarvey, his name was, he came from St Mirren, where he'd been very successful. And I remember Bob Paisley [the then Liverpool manager] telling me that the boy just wasn't up to it. He couldn't deal with the dressing room, with the whole swirl of what it meant to be asked to be hard enough to cope with that.'

McIlvanney also spoke of 'the bullying that goes on. It's a terrible problem if managers don't watch it. The man I regard as the greatest manager ever – Jock Stein [under whom, in 1967, Celtic became the first British winners of the European Cup] – used to watch and if he saw a clique building he'd break it up, because he was stronger than anyone… I'm not saying that it's savage in many instances, but in some it is; you know what they're like, it's a retarded adolescence for many of those guys.'

You wonder what Stein would have made of the power structure at Real Madrid. Steve McManaman described to me the cast-iron hierarchy that he'd found on his arrival. 'I knew that the Spanish players ran the dressing room', he said. 'When I got there Manolo Sanchis was the club captain, and what he said went, and then Hierro took over from him, and then Raul from him. But I was fine. I mean, they were not horrible to anyone. It's just that they set the rules, and we went by them .... I mean, they're the bosses. They looked after everyone. They were the ones who went to the president, they were the ones who went to the manager and said we're not doing this, we're not doing that ... I mean, the players over in Spain are much, much more powerful than the players in England. It's ten times worse in Spain. I mean, that's why they chop and change so much, because the managers have no say, and if the players don't like them, they're out.'

It's difficult to imagine Brian Clough or Sir Alex Ferguson revelling in such an environment. Evidently, McManaman had the twin gifts of diplomacy and understatement, and it's probably those that helped him to negotiate the potential perils of the dressing room. Paul Kimmage, interviewing McManaman for *The Sunday Times*, had picked up on his equanimity, and had tried to find out the dirt: that's to say, what McManaman really thought of a dressing room that could hold Europe's finest managers to ransom. It hadn't, after all, been apparent from *El Macca*, of which Kimmage had observed, 'One of the frustrations of the book is that we don't really get a sense of what makes you tick. But that suited you, didn't it?' McManaman had replied, 'Very much so. I didn't want an autobiography, didn't want to do all that. Maybe people want a bit more insight or wanted me to criticise more, but that's not my style.'

Reading the article, you almost shook your head wearily at the futility of Kimmage's attempt to unlock McManaman's psyche. The Scouser's earnest and inscrutable responses reminded me of the days of boarding school, where you never fell out with someone unless you absolutely had to; it was best to keep your counsel, since the public school network was such a small world that you were bound to run into someone that you'd bad-mouthed sooner or later. It took a certain confidence to hold yourself in like that, and after speaking with McManaman I came to think that this must have been his greatest attribute as a player, superior even to the fine technique with which he'd scored decisive goals in the late stages of the UEFA Champions League. As he'd sat patiently and worked through my set of questions, which I'd slaved over late into the previous evening but which now seemed more banal with each passing moment, I saw that he was uniquely self-assured. As Robbie Fowler wrote of him in his autobiography:

> He's a much more private person than me and far more self-contained. You never really know what he's thinking, and he always has this screen for the outside world. He can speak to anyone, but he won't let his guard down to hardly anybody.

McManaman, who'd grown up on a council estate but with an Old Etonian's mentality, was therefore well prepared for professional football, a world whose actors are constantly probing here and there for any available chinks in your armour. In *Only a Game?* Eamon Dunphy wrote that 'you always have a scapegoat ... When the stars have one of their "serious stuff" moods, they'll often pick on an apprentice and make his life a misery from the moment he makes a mistake. Which is bad. It can ruin a kid, because they can be really cruel.'

Dunphy practised the ostracism that he preached. He'd singled out Gordon Hill, a young left-footed winger of poise and promise, for particularly ruthless abuse. Hill had been only seventeen when he joined Millwall's first team, and hadn't endeared himself to Dunphy and the other senior professionals by what they perceived as his overconfidence. To take him down several pegs, or perhaps to break his spirit – and Dunphy's actions suggest a recklessness as to their effect – several members of Millwall's playing staff were very creative in their cruelty towards Hill. A long-running prank of theirs was to call Hill and pretend to be members of the press, and then encourage him to criticise his teammates; this information would be relayed back to the dressing room, where Hill would face more ridicule than ever.

It seems a trivial matter now, since things worked out well for Hill: he went on to play with Manchester United, winning the 1977 FA Cup against soon-to-be European champions Liverpool, and scoring 51 goals in 131 games in his Old Trafford career. He also won a handful of caps for England as a full international. But that success was due only to the strength of Hill's ego, and when I called him in McKinney, Texas – where he was now coaching a youth team, United FC – he was quick to remind me that others wouldn't have been so fortunate.

Oh my gosh, it was vicious. You're in the deep end. Big time. And you've got to swim. I knew there were a lot of players in the first team that resented me. And, you know, you're in the cold, hard part of London, [where] you shake their hands and clamp your fingers .... I had to win them over, I had to win their respect.

And he did that; though Dunphy was still infuriated by Hill's performances, which fluctuated between the inspired and the indifferent, he was impressed by his unshakeable self belief. Hill, whom the fans nicknamed Merlin in recognition of his magical displays, spoke of Dunphy with animation if not warmth. 'I always found Eamon to be picking at people, picking, picking', said Hill; 'he was a footballing cat-weasel. I mean, he always had something to say, he was never short of a word. He used to go on TV and argue with politicians, that's the sort of person he was. If there was a red fly, he'd say it was a black fly.'

Dunphy went on to a successful career in journalism and television, a world where his trenchant opinions have been more gladly received, whilst Hill went on to ply his trade as part of the Manchester United generation that succeeded the European champions of 1967. Although he was in a team that included men such as Alex Stepney, Steve Coppell and Martin Buchan, players of no small stature themselves, each of that United eleven were aware of the greatness that had gone immediately

114

before them. No one was more taken by that sense of history than Hill, who found a way to stymie the doubt that had infected the thoughts of Raphael Burke. 'When I went to United, they thought I was a very cocky Londoner', he said, 'but I wasn't cocky. People hide their [lack of] confidence in different ways. I hid mine by being arrogant, and I had to, because I'd sit there and I had to pinch myself sometimes that I was sitting in the same changing rooms as the legends once were. I'm thinking, your Denis Laws, your Bobby Charltons, your Tommy Taylors, they've all been in that bath! I mean, it's like visiting a castle and knowing that Henry VIII walked on those steps!'

His point was vividly made – a man who's beheaded two of his wives is a hard act to follow. Hill's mental toughness was essential in negotiating the challenges at Old Trafford and elsewhere in the game. Daniel Spayne, one of the respondents to my survey, was of a similar mind. 'Without self-belief nothing else really matters', he wrote. 'When you look back at the history of football you can see many great players not perform for a variety of reasons but self-doubt would be right up there as one of the key reasons. This is something which can also spread like contagion amongst teammates and can destroy a team's season or cup competition.'

In contrast, self-doubt and Alan Shearer were not well acquainted, as Vic Wakeling reminded me. 'His mental strength was amazing', recalled Wakeling. 'I saw him at seventeen, eighteen, when he first came into the Southampton team, and the first time you saw him [you thought he was] not particularly big, or skilful, if you compared his skills with those who were around then and those who are around today; but he had a great eye for the game. He knew what he was good at, he knew where he was going to be, and then when he got [the ball] he was single-minded, he was mentally tough … he's another one who worked at his game and made the best of the skill he had. I know that I keep going on about George Best, but in the days of the Premiership he has probably been the person who has made a bigger impression on me – at Southampton, Blackburn and Newcastle United – than anyone else.' This was high praise indeed, but as Wakeling pointed out, there had been a famous

Scotsman who'd given the Geordie forward a greater compliment. 'Alex Ferguson will always say that [he was] "the only player I tried twice to sign"', said Wakeling. 'Anybody else, if he tried to sign them and they said no, he never went back. He went back for Shearer.'

Given his admiration for Keegan and Shearer, I suggested to Wakeling that, to be a great player, it was as important to know your limits as it was to know your strengths. 'I think you're absolutely right', he said. 'I also think that someone like Shearer could fit into the Barcelona team of today; into Arsène Wenger's team, Mourinho might have a little debate about whether he'd play Drogba or Shearer up front.' (Although, personally, I couldn't have imagined Alan Shearer in his prime being content on the Chelsea bench.) Here was also a player whose style of play would work well in any era, thought Wakeling, who could have played alongside Bolton's and England's Nat Lofthouse as well as he had played in the modern day.

Shearer had the quality of toughness in abundance; and one vital aspect of toughness is the cruel streak. Football is no stranger to military analogies – a midfielder who directs play is a *general*, a fine striker is a *lethal* finisher, whilst the German team, like all elite armies, is *efficient* – but the quality that it truly reveres has a link with petty crime. Valued above all in football is the ability to be a thief.

Gerd Müller was '*Der Bomber*', showing both the Germans' willingness to enjoy their own perceived militarism and their inaccuracy of expression. Müller was a thief, but he was no bomber; bombers, by definition, make long bombing runs, but Müller didn't waste his time with anything of that variety. His runs were short, frequent, furtive; he scurried about the penalty box like a grave-robber, nicking a half-chance here, a backpass there, leading, among several outstanding feats of goalscoring, to 68 goals in 62 international matches. His most profitable act of theft came in the 1974 World Cup final when, on the stroke of half-time, he swivelled onto a low cross in the area and smuggled it home with a sharp poke of his right foot for a 2–1 lead over Holland. In that moment, which was to decide the match, he'd shoplifted the trophy from the Dutch, a team whose line-up was so gifted – Rob Rensenbrink,

116

Johan Neeskens, Johan Cruyff – that they must have felt almost entitled to victory. But Müller was having none of it, and that's what toughness is all about; you and your opponent will both enter the field of play with the same set of dreams, but in order to leave the field with your set, you've got to want to steal his.

Guts

In the eternal melodrama that is professional football, there are two types of pantomime villain: those players who are tough, and those who are gutsy. To be a great player, you've got to have a foot in both camps, between which the distinction is ultimately a simple one: the tough are those who give it, and the gutsy are those who go looking for it. In a sense, it's this latter group of players who truly shape the game of football. They're the ones for whom opposition fans have a peculiar affection, a special place in their hearts for personal and profound loathing.

The supporters, then, have a hate figure around whom they can unite. But that's not to say that the gutsy player doesn't gain from this anti-hero status – there are several of them who seem to find the hatred from the stands almost nutritious. Certainly, John Collins considered this vitriol to be a wholesome meal: he told me that part of the fun in football was scoring in a big match away from home, knowing that you were directly responsible for the resentful silence of eighty per cent of those watching you.

Fiorentina's Gabriel Batistuta felt this just as strongly. After a sensational strike against Barcelona in the Nou Camp – an eruption from his right foot that had the goalkeeper ducking for cover – he ran towards the crowd of one-hundred-and-twenty-thousand and pressed his fingers to his lips. Batistuta, having rendered the atmosphere in the stadium more joyless than that of a coffin, shouldn't have been so complacent that he'd survive the experience. The Nou Camp faithful are notorious for their rage when their faith has been betrayed, or their patience unduly stretched. Luis Figo, when he moved from Barcelona to Real Madrid, famously found himself the target of not only horrific abuse but also mobile phones and the head of a suckling pig, each of which were rained down towards him as he approached the pitch. The rationale for throw-

119

ing the pork missile was unclear: its originator may have been making the point that pigs might fly before Figo was again welcome in that football ground. Nevertheless, Figo manfully endured this trial by fire.

The Portuguese great also illustrated an important point, although he might not have been grateful for doing so at the time: that it takes a very special kind of personality to absorb all of the emotion that's poured into the recipe of a football match. Guts are therefore a skill as vital as a sound first touch. They're an invisible muscle that can put the body under more strain than any arduous weight session, and, from time to time, even the strongest may fail to carry themselves. Marcel Desailly, watching Zinedine Zidane as France approached the 1998 World Cup final, asked himself if one man 'could withstand so much passion': Zidane, then the obsession of a nation, had been sent off for an apparently needless stamp on a Saudi Arabian player in the group stages.

But Zidane had one important aspect in his favour: he had size, and many of the gutsiest players don't have that luxury. Small, mobile and precise of touch, they're a threat to the status quo. No hard man likes to be outfoxed by a deft, diminutive opponent; there's a fear that he'll have his manhood undermined. What's more, there's a deep-seated feeling in football that the small players won't pull their weight when it really matters. Accusations of this sort will have hung over the head of Juninho when he arrived at Middlesbrough from Sao Paulo in 1995, having been voted the Brazilian player of the year in the previous year. Juninho, at five feet five inches in height, had a series of doubters, many of whom were asking an earlier version of what should now be known as the 'Freddy Adu question'. The United States' Freddy Adu, another small player and a prodigy who has drawn hasty comparisons with Pelé for the precocity of his talent, undertook a two-week trial at Manchester United in the autumn of 2006. Much like Juninho, he possessed a hypnotic dribble and a good reading of the game; but there was a suggestion that he might not be mentally ready, or gutsy enough, for the rigours of the Premiership. The question was memorably phrased by Adu's technical coach at DC United, one Dave Kasper: 'Does Freddy want to have to go to Watford on a rainy Wednesday where he'll have six-foot-four goons on his back all night?'

In 1995, there was no shortage of hard men to ask Juninho the Freddy Adu question, but he answered it emphatically, soon being named the top division's player of the year. Gerrard has noted a similar resilience in Cristiano Ronaldo's predecessor on the Portuguese wing, Luis Figo. In his autobiography, Gerrard commented: 'I thought I knew everything about the great Figo – technique, pure class on the ball – but I didn't realise how strong he was … Whack Figo, he comes back for more. Whack him again, he gets up and runs back at you. Figo possesses the quality I call moral courage. Even when he's battered and bruised, he has the heart to keep going. What a legend.'

Luis Figo, the FIFA World Player of the Year in 2001, was desperate for the ball when the game was at its pivotal point; there are many others who'd have gladly shirked possession at such a time, preferring the closely-related comforts of anonymity and mediocrity. Simon Barnes wrote of their mentality, of their 'fear of being put to the test: a fear not of other people but of oneself. Not exactly a fear of failure, no, nor even a fear of success. Rather, a fear of the process of testing: a fear of being found wanting, of being found out.'

George Best, in contrast, embraced that process, secure as he was in the knowledge that he'd humiliate his examiner. As Vic Wakeling observed, 'Everyone knows about George's skills, but actually George – and there was no size to him whatsoever, he was slightly built, of no great height, he wasn't as tall as me – was a guy who tackled back, who was kicked all over the park by some very hard defenders such as Graham Williams at West Brom, and he kept getting up and going in for more. But he also tackled back as well, so if he saw a head-on challenge he'd never try and jump over it, he'd take it on and try and win the ball. And a lot of the time he did. And I think, for a player of that type of skill, he was quite unique.'

Gutsy players will constantly test the temperaments of the crowd, the opponents, their teammates, and of course themselves: especially themselves. They involve everyone in what is, truthfully, a pretty sadistic process. Robbie Savage, in his Birmingham City days, in his Leicester City days, in his Blackburn – in fact, wherever he's played – has managed to create one of the more unpleasant on-pitch personas in the game. A yelping, spiteful blond scarecrow, scampering his scrawny way about the midfield, he defied anyone who watched or played with him not so much to love or hate him, but rather to be indifferent to his presence. Few were sufficiently patient to achieve that state of mind; yet, in a TV documentary, he was genuinely bemused by the amount of opprobrium that he'd attracted. To him, it was all pantomime.

In this vein, he has much in common with Cristiano Ronaldo, who's now thankfully renowned more for his quick feet than for his folly: or, as Gordon Hill referred to them, 'his tartish manners'. Hill, it must be said, wasn't above cheek himself. 'I remember I was at Old Trafford, I get the ball and who do I nutmeg but Norman Hunter', he told me, with more than a remnant of relish. 'And I heard Hunter saying, "If you ever fucking do that to me again, son, I'll break both your legs." Typical Londoner, I just turned round and laughed; I said, "Fuck off, you've got to be joking", and just ran off. And Norman Hunter didn't speak to me for about ten years. But I didn't care. I wasn't there to make defenders look good.'

Yet another of Ronaldo's forebears – this time David Beckham, in the number-seven shirt at Manchester United – has shown that whilst there's much that is naïve about the gutsy, there's also much that is noble. To paraphrase the old saying: there are those who are born being gutsy, and those who have being gutsy thrust upon them. In his autobiography, Sir Alex Ferguson wrote almost movingly – for him, at least – of Beckham's resolve under pressure; when the chips were down, said Ferguson, Beckham would not be found wanting. Never was this more in evidence than in 1999, in the season following David Beckham's sending-off against Argentina in the 1998 World Cup. Effigies of Beckham were burnt in the street, as England, that most secular of nations, conducted a witch-hunt with impressively religious fervour. Vicious insults were spat from the mouths of fans around the country. And Beckham had the season of his life.

Beckham crossed the ball so well that season that his own highlight videos became cliché: it seemed that the same scene happened endlessly, the only differences the shirts of the opposition that he swerved the ball beyond. Each time, again and again: the outside rim of his right boot ruffling the white hair of the touchline as he drew it back, then the smooth, savage downswing, clipping the ball smartly across its gut, sending it soaring to the head of a striker who too soared to meet it. That he found such exceptional form as Manchester United made their way to a treble of Premiership, FA Cup and European Champions League is powerful demonstration of one thing: that whilst Beckham's status as a truly great player is debated with perhaps telling regularity, his courage has never been in doubt.

Courage: something that's needed for one of the loneliest places in the sporting world, which is the football pitch during a penalty shootout; in fact, there's a strong case for the argument that it's the loneliest of all. It's probably the loneliest because football's the only major sport that decides its contests with such a brutal immediacy: one shot. Because of this instant method of conflict resolution, the shootout has been somewhat lazily compared to Russian roulette. Johann Cruyff has spoken of the haplessness of the penalty-taker's predicament. In an interview with Frits Barend and Henk van Dorp, he explained that 'the penalty is a speciality and it doesn't have any direction with football … the thing is that a penalty seems to be very easy, which is why it's very difficult.' With this in mind, he went on to discuss the technique that the sensible player should adopt in the penalty shootout: 'Close your eyes really tight, and ask God's blessing.'

This may have been Holland's policy in the Euro 2000 semi-final against Italy, but in any event it was a disastrous one. Zenden, not without some unresolved pain ringing through his voice, relived the moment for me. (Later that season, Zenden was to score in a shootout against Chelsea as Liverpool went through to the final of the 2007 UEFA Champions League, but neither of us were to know that then.) 'De Boer missed the first one, Kluivert hit the post on the second; and then, during the shootout, we had five kicks, of which we missed three. Bosvelt missed, and de Boer again … '. How about Stam, I asked. The former Manchester United defender had sent his penalty soaring into the Amsterdam evening. Zenden gave an amused sigh. 'As for Stam's miss, they're still looking for that one.'

A common complaint from footballers is that penalties require no skill, that even the most technically-gifted players are likely to miss. That's a snobbish argument, since it implies that the most entertaining side deserves to win any given match; but, in any event, maybe a question about levels of skill isn't what the penalty shootout is asking. Simon Barnes has referred to the shootout as 'a phrase that is called – closer to a literal description than a metaphor – sudden death'; he has also written that 'it is a fact that penalty competitions are unfair. They are melodramatic crap-shoots and they take place because football has sold its birthright for a mess of television money. It's great telly but it's a lottery that mocks at the sincerity of the players. All sport takes place in the theatre of cruelty but the penalty shootout, like the bullring, is the theatre of gratuitous cruelty.'

There are several respects in which football has been commercially exploited to breaking point. But to refer to the shootout as a lottery is, to lapse briefly into pedantry, historically inaccurate. It was the system which preceded the shootout that was the true lottery, games of the greatest significance being decided by the toss of a coin. So went the 1964–5 European Cup quarter-final between Liverpool and Cologne, and the semi-final of the 1968 European Championships between Italy and the Soviet Union. Billy McNeill, the captain of the 1967 Celtic team that was the first British side to win the European Cup, has spoken in disparaging terms of this procedure. In an interview with BBC Sport, he described the scene when Benfica and Celtic awaited the outcome of a coin toss to settle their 1969 European Cup quarter-final. 'The toss of a coin was a farcical way of deciding quarter-finals – irrespective of who won. It was done in the referee's room … all the players waiting there for the result were apprehensive … After it was decided, it was chaos. I didn't speak to any of the Benfica players instantly afterwards, but I knew they were angry.' Angry may have been an understatement. Agonising as it is, the shootout is less so than what has gone before; at least now the players' courage is put to the test, whereas before the only test was fate.

The creator of the shootout, the German referee Karl Wald, is rightly unrepentant about his invention. (Although, given the success that his nation has enjoyed in this format, there is the suspicion that he may have given them advance warning of his plans, so that they could all go away and practise in advance.) 'It's the only way in which a result can be achieved fairly', he told the *Kerala News*. 'Everything else was not really a solution. I always believed I was right.' In any event, what's beyond doubt is that there's nothing more revealing of someone's character than if they are ready to step up to the spot or not: and to be unwilling marks one out, fairly or not, as something of a coward.

Maybe that's why Roberto Baggio, Daniele Massaro and Baresi weren't reviled in Italy when they missed from the spot in the 1994 World Cup final, the first match of that scale to have been resolved in this fashion. Baggio, for his part, seems to have been vaguely aware of his appointment with destiny well in advance. As he told *The Observer Sport Monthly*, 'Before I left for the finals, my Buddhist spiritual master told me that I would be confronted with a lot of problems and that everything would be decided at the very last minute. At the time I didn't realise that his prediction would be so accurate.' Baggio identifies that miss, unsurprisingly, as the worst moment of his career. He argues that 'losing a World Cup final on penalties is not right ... is it right that four years of sacrifice are decided by three minutes of penalties? I don't think so. Losing that way isn't right, and neither is winning that way.' There's a whole other debate to be had about the validity of the penalty shootout; but, as Stuart Pearce has showed with both his failure and success in this discipline, what takes real guts is not scoring from the spot, but stepping up to it.

It's at this point that we should pause, having discussed at almost excessive length the failures or triumphs of nerve of many an outfield player, and we should pay homage to the goalkeeper. The goalkeeper is often looked upon as crazy, and there'll be a fuller examination of his sanity in the chapter on Madness, but for now he should be praised for his own particular brand of courage. Often he'll find himself with his head down in the path of onrushing forwards as he dives to claim the ball, and for them such hazardous activity is routine; one of the finest goalkeepers, Manchester City's Bert Trautmann, even played the 1956 FA Cup Final with a broken neck. (In fact, Trautmann, as a German living in England shortly after World War Two, had shown great resolve just by daring to enter the country.)

The best of a brave bunch, though, and therefore worthy of his own couple of paragraphs, is Lev Yashin; despite Peter Schmeichel's formidable claims to that title, the Russian remains the only goalkeeper to have been named European Footballer of the Year. What's more, the Dynamo Moscow goalkeeper was crowned in 1963, ahead of a particularly fine array of attacking talent: Denis Law, Eusebio, Gianni Rivera and Jimmy Greaves were all lurking enviously in the ranks of the runners-up. The 'Black Spider', as he was known, relished the one-on-one confrontation with the striker more than any other, and was estimated to have saved over one-hundred-and-fifty penalty kicks in his lifetime. The footage of him that survives is elegant, but elusive; and so, during the course of my research, I was forced to look elsewhere for fitting tributes. One website which offered its own shrine to the Russian was www.beatyashin.com. 'Lev Yashin was one of the greatest goalkeepers in the history of football', it told me, and then gave me a challenge: 'Now is your chance to beat Lev Yashin, in a penalty shootout.' Having enjoyed his brief highlights, and keen to see what he was made of, I agreed. There was even a football shirt on offer if you netted enough penalties; I entered the site and started the game, pointing and clicking the mouse at the ball so that I could somehow slip it past this cartoon rendering of the greatest goalkeeper ever.

Yashin must have been turning in his grave; even if you blasted the thing straight at his chest the ball went in, and I scored ten goals before I started feeling disrespectful. Slightly embarrassed at how smug this victory had made me feel, I moved on, and found a better example of his legacy. Living at a time when the primary obsession of many of his fellow Russians had been the space race, to blast one of their own men beyond

126

the atmosphere before those cursed Americans could do it, Yashin retained an admirable sense of his priorities. 'The joy of seeing Yuri Gagarin flying in space', he said, a true football man, 'is only superseded by the joy of a good penalty save.'

Whether a player has balls, guts, bottle, *chutzpah*, *cojones* – or whatever you choose to call the opposite of cowardice – isn't a precise science. Courage on the football pitch is generally assessed over time: it's rare that a footballer will be judged for the whole of his career on the basis of one moment. And that's right, because to condemn a player as lacking heart is to question that quality on which he may pride himself most of all; it shouldn't be a judgement lightly made.

But, too often, it's a judgement falsely made, one that may arise over little but then acquire devastating momentum. Eamon Dunphy has written that 'you get what amounts to a whispering campaign starting about a player. And the longer the whispering campaign goes on, the more convincing the argument becomes. Even to the point of totally ignoring reality ... these little whisperings emerge that have no basis in fact at all.' Dunphy continues: 'Crowds do it ... "So-and-so is a wanker – is a wanker – is a wanker", and no way, short of scoring a hat-trick each week for six weeks, can he get rid of that.'

Thierry Henry has suffered from what you might call Chinese whispers, or what – in an attempt to be humorous – I've called 'Highbury's whispers'. The campaign that Henry has faced is a concerted one, whose chief contention has hardened, in many minds, into irrefutable fact: that he can't score in big games. A 'big game', in plenty of which Henry has played, is generally a Cup final. He's played in three FA Cup finals, in 2001, 2002 and 2003, against Liverpool, Chelsea and Southampton; a UEFA Cup final, in 2000, against Galatasaray; a UEFA Champions League final, in 2005, against Barcelona; a European Championship final, against Italy in 2002; and a World Cup final, again against Italy, in 2006. And, as is widely known – and as he's all too readily reminded – he's failed to hit the target in any of them.

Seven major finals, only three winners' medals, no goals; all but one of these games decided by a goal at most; three games going, at least, to extra time; two of those games ending in defeat on penalties. Matches this close were crying out for this world-class forward to assert himself. Henry's record sits uncomfortably alongside that of Sweden's Henrik Larsson, for too many years an underrated player, who incidentally provided two crucial assists in that 2005 UEFA Champions League final to win the trophy for Barcelona. Henry, earlier, had passed up two reasonable opportunities. Supporters of Henry, those who say that he has guts, will argue that these were matches in which he was policed more tightly than the gates of the Vatican: that his movement drew defenders, allowing him to usher lesser threats towards goal, so that they could be decisive.

But those who resist Henry's legend would counter that the great players salivate over these opportunities; to paraphrase the novelist Tibor Fischer, they'd thrive on such adversity like a slap-up meal. It's on days and nights like these, in the midst of contests of such fine balance and terrific intensity, that the Frenchman should truly have stepped away from his supporting cast. Of course, a big game is also a vital Premiership or Champions League match, and Henry has found the net in plenty of those, but the charge sheet remains a daunting one. Seven major finals, no goals. Highbury's whispers have persisted to such an extent that they'd influence several people to deny Henry a place among the greats.

Of course, Henry has done much in his career other than to fail to score in close-run finals, enough, you would have thought, to have earned sufficient goodwill to fend off attacks on his nerve for the big occasion. There are the two Premiership titles, the two European Golden Boots, the three Football Writers' awards, not to mention the small matter of a European Championship and a World Cup winner's medal. But then there are the Highbury's whispers, which claim that Henry was only truly in his pomp when playing at home, at Arsenal's old north-London ground. The reasoning was that he failed to score frequently enough away from home, whereas being able to do so was the mark of a real striker. Or perhaps a real man; and maybe Henry's the wrong kind of man. There's so much that seems effortless in his play, whilst in English football, so much must be conspicuous. A player must be seen to have worked his socks off, to have sweated blood, and his heart must be clearly visible on his sleeve. The nation as a whole only truly warmed to David Beckham when, in 2002, he ran over ten miles in a game against Greece, as if that distance was some kind of receipt against which he could offset his more effete tendencies.

Like Beckham, Henry's work rate is prodigious, as is his team ethic; but there's still something a little too pretty about him. Maybe that's where the suspicion about his guts emerged from, long before he had any trouble in the first of those major finals. He may have been regarded as too conscious of fashion to do the less than dainty things that all of the great finishers must occasionally do: to bundle the ball home from three yards, to poke the ball past the goalkeeper in a goalmouth scramble, to score the ugly goal. To his detractors, Henry's literally afraid to get his knees dirty; his socks are hoisted high up over them, so that even when he slides to celebrate a score they stay free from the taint of the turf, innocent until proven filthy.

If we can, we'll put those seven major finals to one side, and concentrate merely on the Premiership – as many of Henry's fiercest critics are wont to do – to examine his domestic goalscoring record. It's a fine one, but to see how much guts Henry really has, we should set it alongside that of someone who even the least primal of instincts would recognise as a real man, Newcastle's Alan Shearer. Shearer struck the ball as if you were awarded extra points for bursting it. As a friend of mine observed, as we were comparing the Frenchman and the Englishman, 'Shearer seems to hit the ball with the laces. Henry side-foots it.' Maybe that would've been the difference, the laces against the instep, the force against the finesse, in those seven major finals.

The difference wasn't so apparent from their resumés. I took the first seven seasons that both strikers had spent in the Premiership: Henry had scored 0.65 goals per game, a total of 154, an average slightly behind Shearer, who recorded the gaudy tally of 153 goals at 0.70 goals per game. The common criticism of Henry was that he couldn't score away from home; this was investigated by the analysts who supply statistics for the Opta Jury, a feature on the Sky Sports website that subjects footballing assumptions to numerical scrutiny. They found that 'indeed, 114 of Henry's 165 Premiership goals are now just memories at the club's abandoned home [of Highbury] and there has only ever been one Premiership season when Henry has scored as many goals on the road as he has at home.'

What the statisticians failed to note, however, is that all of the very best strikers – including Henry – have considerably greater difficulty scoring away than they do at home. An Englishman's home is his castle, after all, and he isn't just going to let any old Frenchman walk into it on a cold Wednesday night and walk away with a world-class hat-trick. In the period that we're looking at, Henry scored just under a third – or 32% – of his goals away from home, which suggests that an away goal, as recognised by European competition in the event of a tie, is indeed twice as hard to come by as a goal scored at home. In the same time span, Alan Shearer managed to score 44 of his goals away from home, or 29%.

Henry's numbers aren't, so far, those of someone gutless. They stand comfortably alongside those of Shearer who in that seven-year period between 1992 and 1999 was at the peak of his game, winning one league title with Blackburn Rovers and almost winning another with Newcastle. Shearer and Henry are also inseparable in another respect: they scored roughly the same proportion of goals before and after half-time, meaning that they represented constant threats throughout the entire match. Both players, in fact, were marginally more dangerous in the second half than in the first, Henry scoring 56% after half-time, with Shearer recording a similar figure of 53%.

But, of course, you can prove almost anything with statistics; you could argue just as easily that the best strikers, the gutsiest ones, score early when the game is goalless and there for the taking. But if you argued that on the above facts, you'd be on thin intellectual ice, and you'd really just be looking for reasons to criticise Henry. But, as discussed earlier, you can't prove the existence or absence of guts with mere figures. This is the world of Highbury's whispers, where different rules apply, and the two crucial facts seem to be these: first, that the statisticians behind the Opta Jury never felt the need to put the minutiae of Shearer's record under the microscope, instinctively reassured as they were of the certainty of his finishing; and, second, that Alan Shearer never wore his socks above his knees.

As Henry knows all too well, the player whose watchword is elegance will always face accusations that he lacks nerve. We started this discussion with Juninho's escape from that stereotype, and so, in the interests of symmetry, we'll finish this chapter with the contrast of two more flamboyant forwards, Brazil's Bebeto and Luis Figo. Vialli, no stranger to flair himself, had written in *The Italian Job* of guts, of 'the truly intangible quality, the one I'll call "balls".' He commented that 'there are players who hide in crucial moments. They don't want to take responsibility so they won't show for a pass or they won't make a run, fearing what might happen if they receive the ball and make a mistake.'

There are some players who hide at moments so important that it marks their entire careers, and almost certainly bars them from the ranks of the great. Brazil's Bebeto must be classed as one such. In the 1993–4 season his club side, Deportivo La Coruna, threatened to break the hold of Barcelona and Real Madrid over the Spanish league; with a single game to go, this Galician team were only a victory away from the championship. In that final game, with the score 0–0, Deportivo were awarded a penalty in the final minute. But Bebeto refused to take it. He made this refusal despite being the league's leading goalscorer, or *Pichichi*, from the previous season; and despite the fact that the regular penalty-taker, Donato, had already left the field. The responsibility then fell to Miroslav Djukić, a defender, who made such weak contact with his penalty that the goalkeeper was able to fall slowly forward and engulf the ball with his arms. Barcelona Catalans took the championship, and Djukić is still cruelly referred to by some as their player of the season for that year. Bebeto, meanwhile, sealed his legacy as merely a superb player, and not a great one; if that penalty had been offered to Luis Figo he'd have snatched the opportunity, and that's the difference.

Madness

Bill Parcells, the legendary coach of the New York Giants American football team, knew about madness. Simon Barnes told me the story:

> He was being questioned on the eve of the 1986 Super Bowl, I think it was, about some touchline fisticuffs that he'd had with one of his players. Parcells refused to confirm or deny reports of the fight, but instead held up his hand to stop the reporters' questions, and said: 'Look. This is not a game for well-adjusted people.'

Whether or not you're a football fan, you must accept that there's something unhinged – if not entirely crazy – about twenty-two men chasing a ball. It's an accusation often casually made, but consider it calmly for a moment. Twenty-two grown men, at 7.45 p.m. on a chilly November night or at 3.00 p.m. under a scorching August sun, kitted out in flimsy and synthetic threads for ninety minutes of conflict. They're waiting for a balding middle-aged man to blow his whistle, and thus release them in pursuit of a small, white synthetic sphere. Just fifteen minutes ago, that same sphere had sagged sad and empty, unnoticed on a dressing room bench; now, proud and pumped, primed, it's the obsession of forty-four feet, of several thousand fans in that stadium, and several million watching elsewhere. Professional football is crazy.

It's logical, then, that those who ply their trade in this world should have a healthy streak of madness; and the better they are, the madder they'll be. So when Zinedine Zidane threw away the 2006 World Cup with his extra-time head-butt on Italy's Marco Materazzi, onlookers should not have been so surprised. That's just the kind of insanity that they should've expected from football.

In fact, insanity might not be the right word. 'Sane', as defined in the

133

Penguin Dictionary (2nd edition), means 'able to anticipate and assess the effects of one's actions': technically speaking, there's nothing insane about what Zidane did. When he decided to attack Materazzi – his only lasting regret being, perhaps, that he failed to make more emphatic contact – the option to head-butt the Inter Milan defender presented itself with brilliant clarity. At that time, it was the only rational response to the tension within; so to call it a moment of madness is a nice piece of alliteration, but it comfortably misses the point. Professional footballers subject themselves to scenarios at which ordinary civilians would baulk: they frequently end up in situations of tremendous pressure that can only be resolved in terms of black and white, by becoming hero or villain. It's unnatural, for example, to gamble the entire legacy of your career on a small white spot twelve yards from goal, as you do when you approach the ball in a penalty shootout.

It's natural, then, that Zidane should have cracked when he did. In that calm split second, he became what the novelist Kurt Vonnegut, writing in a different context, called 'appallingly human': he reminded us that there was only a man inside that number-ten shirt after all. In some respects, he even reassured us that football is only a game. As he trudged back towards the dressing room, past the World Cup perched haughtily on its dais, he didn't even glance at the trophy he'd clutched eight years before. And as he loomed over it, and then moved beyond it, the trophy suddenly looked not quite so imposing, nor quite so golden.

But we're happy to keep our footballers crazy, since madness so often rouses and inspires us. This love affair with the tortured artist reaches far back into earlier societies. The late Professor Roy Porter, in his *Madness: A Brief History*, observed that 'Greek thinkers advanced the idea of divine madness in the artist, "inspired" (literally "filled with spirit") or touched by a divine fire. Notably in the Phaedrus, Plato spoke of the "divine fury" of the poet.' It's possible that the notoriously fiery Eric Cantona shared this notion, naming his fellow countryman and poet, Rimbaud, as one of his greatest influences. It's not clear whether the Leeds and Manchester United showman was entirely unpretentious in this claim: but the fact that he made his delight in poetry so public, in a sport that aggressively resists the more feminine elements of nature, shows football's acceptance that its most creative players are allowed to be that little bit different.

Madness often drives its victims to change the world around them for better or worse: as Porter also noted, 'Holy innocents, prophets, ascetics, and visionaries too might be possessed by a "good madness". But derangement was more commonly viewed as diabolic, schemed by Satan and spread by witches and heretics.' Derangement – or 'bad madness', as a medieval inquisitor might have termed it – among footballers is sometimes so exhilarating that we accept this as part of the general package of genius. For example, while there was outrage in 1995 when Cantona launched a kick at the chest of a Crystal Palace supporter, there was also a primal, visceral pride amongst some supporters, similar to the reaction that Zidane received after the 2006 World Cup final. In his rage, Cantona had vented his frustration at this fan, who had been hurling obscene insults, in a way that some found almost thrilling: thrilling enough, in Zidane's case, to inspire a number-one single (*Coupe de Boule*, or 'Headbutt') in the French charts.

The recurring belief in a footballer's madness as both a divine gift and curse suggests that football isn't all that secular a sport. There's an almost spiritual streak in many footballers and fans that sees players as the channels for heavenly intentions: most infamously, Maradona sought refuge in the 'Hand Of God' to justify his instinctive and decisive cheating against England in the 1986 World Cup in Mexico. Greats in other sports and arts have also discussed this sense of being 'unconscious', or, in American parlance, 'in the zone': where, at the same moment that they feel most imperious, they feel as if some other unseen force is guiding them, and, as a result, they are moved, even frightened by their own ability. Such examples are legion, and legendary. For a start, there's Gascoigne's Euro '96 strike against Scotland, featured more fully in the later chapter on Vision. In 2005 Roger Federer, who, since the days of Pete Sampras, is the closest that tennis has come to having an emperor, remarked – a little immodestly – after his third successive Wimbledon title that 'I amaze myself how incredibly I use my talent to win.' In 1991, when the Chicago Bulls met the Portland Trail Blazers in the NBA

Finals, Michael Jordan turned in a first-half display of shooting so awe-some that he shrugged in amusement at the crowd. 'The basket seemed like some big old wash-bucket', he recalled after the game. But perhaps the most lyrical, and enduring, description of this 'unconscious' state was provided by Mozart, as he discussed what went through his mind as he composed. It's so powerful a passage that it should be quoted in full:

> When I feel well and in a good humour, or when I am taking a drive, or walking after a good meal, or in the night when I can not sleep, thoughts crowded my mind as easily as you could wish. Whence and how do they come? I do not know and I have nothing to do with it. Those which please me I keep in my head, and hum, at least others have told me that I do so. Once I have my theme another melody comes, linking itself to the first one, in accordance with the needs of the composition as a whole. The counterpoint, the part of each instrument and all these melodic fragments, at last produce the entire work. Then my soul is on fire with inspiration. The work grows, I keep expanding it, conceiving it more and more clearly, until I have the entire composition finished in my head though it may be long.

When footballers fail to explain perfectly how they scored a particular goal or how they played a particular pass, they are often accused of being inarticulate. But perhaps that's unfair. In the quotation above, it's appar-ent that Mozart in his most sublime moments was 'unconscious': that he didn't know what he was doing other than responding to the instinct that moved him.

In truth, there's at least as much craziness to be found amongst the coaching staff and fans as there is amongst the players. A football stadium is a place where sociopathic behaviour is tolerated, and often revered. As Robbie Fowler once observed, 'It's a funny thing, the hatred you get from the terraces. There are thousands and thousands of people … shouting they're gonna fucking kill you, they're gonna rip your head off and shit in the hole, they're gonna string you up from the roof of the stand ... and they're three feet away behind a knee-high wooden hoarding. You need a sense of humour sometimes, believe me.'

In *The Mourning Bride* William Congreve, in a quote often attributed to Shakespeare, wrote that 'heav'n has no Rage, like Love to Hatred turn'd, nor Hell a Fury, like a Woman scorn'd'. But Congreve wrote that sentence in 1697, and so he never saw the fury of a scorned football fan. Despite the dangerous passions that the sport ignites in too many supporters, the football pitch can be something of a sanctuary. Paul Gascoigne, of course, found it such: he has confessed that 'I suppose I looked upon football as the best cure, the one aspect of my life that has always kept me focused, cleared my head of all my worries and phobias, allowed me to escape from my worst self.' Lee Bowyer was another troubled midfielder who found refuge in football. During the 2001 season, Bowyer stood trial for the assault of Safraz Najeib, a student he was alleged to have beaten savagely outside a nightclub in Leeds. That trial, in which Bowyer was eventually acquitted, coincided with perhaps his best run of form in a Leeds United shirt, as the team went to the semi-finals of the Champions League before falling 3–0 on aggregate to Valencia. 'Bowyer's decision to attend court and then play amazed people around the country', wrote David Batty, 'but it didn't surprise me because I figured it was the best way of finding a release for the incredible pressure he must have been under.'

So Bowyer found his release in football; but escaping the pressures of football itself is another matter. It's thankfully not common for the game to take such a crushing psychological toll. Andy Barton told me that it was very rare that footballers would lose sleep over the huge sums for which they were transferred. But there are isolated and harrowing examples, and sadly, Sebastian Deisler would come to know that all too well. The Bayern Munich midfielder, once hailed as Germany's next great player, retired in 2007 at the age of twenty-seven after a series of injuries. However, the clinical depression from which he suffered hardly helped.

Another less reported but no less tragic case was that of Jan Šimák, the Czech midfielder bought by Bayer Leverkusen to replace Michael Ballack in 2003. Šimák, until then an outstanding playmaker, publicly confessed to fear at stepping into the boots of Ballack, who'd led Leverkusen in the previous season to second place in three domestic and European competitions. Šimák, who as Barton surmised 'probably didn't feel worthy', went absent without leave and was found weeks later in a bar, back in the Czech Republic. He was subsequently diagnosed as suffering from nervous exhaustion, and was released by the German club at the end of the season.

Just under half of those who answered my questionnaire thought that madness was the least important quality of a great footballer. Steve Jeffes considered that Zidane's head-butt was 'just a one off, and I fear you're just trying to get him in to your survey'. Stuart Wakeford, meanwhile, felt that my terminology was a little too stark. 'Not madness – but eccentricity', wrote Wakeford. 'To say that being mad is a requirement of greatness is wrong. I'm sure you don't mean it literally but I think the term is a bit strong. Gascoigne, Maradona, Cantona: all eccentric – but I'm not sure [that] mad is true.'

Wakeford's comment made me wonder whether I'd been flippant in using the term, madness. I'd been trying to capture the explosive obsession that many of the top footballers seem to have with the game, and not for the first time I wondered whether 'passion' would have been a better noun. The Roman playwright Seneca (3BC–AD65) was to blame for much of this debate. He had written, in a phrase roughly translated from the original Latin, that 'no great genius has existed without a strain of madness'. He was following the observation of Aristotle, who during his *Problemata* had asked:

Why is it that all men who have become above average either in philosophy, politics, poetry, or the arts seem to be melancholy, and some to such an extent that they are even seized by the diseases [that result from] black bile?

Zidane was known to vomit on the pitch at times of extreme pressure – for example, before taking a late penalty against England at Euro 2004 –

but to say that he was in the grip of black bile, a medieval and mythical bodily fluid, would be stretching it. At any rate, my survey revealed, the age-old connection between madness and genius was something for which modern football fans had little time; so I looked to more recent examinations of this link.

One of the most elegant is that made by Matthew Parris, a columnist for *The Times*, in an article in 2003. Infamously questioning the sanity of Prime Minister Tony Blair's decision to go to war against Iraq, Parris wrote that 'genius and madness are often allied, and nowhere is this truer than in political leadership. Great leaders need self-belief in unnatural measure. Simple fraudsters are rumbled early, but great leaders share with great confidence tricksters a capacity to be more than persuaded, but inhabited, by their cause. Almost inevitably, an inspirational leader spends important parts of his life certain of the uncertain, convinced of the undemonstrable. So do the mentally ill.'

A less lucid but more forensic analysis than that made by Parris came from Dr Kenneth Lyen of the Singapore Medical Association, in his 2002 paper *Beautiful Minds: Is there a link between genius and madness?* Lyen's study gets off to a cautious start, stating that 'it may be prudent for one not to be sucked into the quicksands that surround the definition of madness'. He subsequently draws attention to the startling 1974 research by Nancy Andreasen of the University of Iowa, 'who studied 30 faculty members attending a writers' workshop and matched them with 30 controls. She found that 80% of participating writers suffered from depression or bipolar disorder, compared to 30% of her controls'. But being more sensitive than a layperson such as myself, who would casually throw phrases like 'football-mad' about my speech, Dr Lyen tentatively observes that 'there is a small body of epidemiological evidence to support a link between creativity and bipolar disorders, but this is not the same as saying between genius and madness'.

It's then that he drifts closer to what Peter Sebastian, in an e-mail to me, identified as the heart of the issue: that much of Maradona's success was 'due to the fact that he had a mad streak, making him completely unpredictable'. Alexis Everington wrote similarly of this spontaneous essence, referring to it as the 'Dark Horse Factor'. Of such a player, Everington asked: 'Will he go left or right, will he pass or drill from 30 yards, will he rinse his opponent or find his neighbour? Commentators desperately try to pin him down into a category but fail. He is a master of disguise, a virtuoso in unpredictability, his expertise in deception would have Sun Tzu for breakfast. Cristiano Ronaldo may reach such dizzy heights, Zidane certainly got there and Ronaldinho virtually defines this quality.' We'll come to Ronaldinho in a moment, but it's more immediately useful to look to Dr Lyen, who has fleshed out this 'Dark Horse' theory. He writes that:

> Certain mental disorders like schizophrenia and bipolar disorder are characterised by sudden jumps in one's thinking. These leaps from one idea to another can be quite unexpected and illogical, and are referred to as Knight's Move Thinking. This way of thinking is important in creative thinking because it enables a person to make innovative leaps without being anchored to preconceived ideas or imprisoned by one's sense of logic.

It's tempting to see these innovative leaps in thinking as Ronaldinho's forte, Barcelona's icon being the master of the devastating last-minute decision. He has said that 'my game is based on improvisation. Often a forward does not have the time to think too much. You have a second, rarely more, to decide whether to dribble, shoot or pass to the right or left. It is instinct that gives the orders.'

But Ronaldinho's thinking doesn't involve 'sudden jumps'; it's not as if his thoughts are scattered all over the place. His state of mind when he plays is closer to Mozart's unconsciousness; it's unthinking, which is the true nature of improvisation. Any useful medical definition of madness doesn't, therefore, apply to him, which is perhaps why most of those that I surveyed chose rightly to reject it. In the cold light of day, it's an unnecessarily cruel word.

But, crucially, it's a word that's used to imply a certain heat of emotion; and so, for the sake of narrative, I can press on with my lazier, layman's definition of madness. Carelessly speaking, madness is that concoction of passion and vision, of wit and compulsion, that makes the great footballers act more instantly than anyone could expect. Thankfully, then, madness can be a thing of great beauty. Long before men had football as an outlet to let off steam, they sank themselves into other, no less vivid, pursuits. The rage of Achilles, in Homer's *Iliad*, is one of the most lyrical descriptions of an athlete's madness to be found anywhere in literature: the Greek hero, his frenzy caused by the death of his closest companion Patroclus, sets about the Trojan enemy with a terrible urgency:

[Achilles] sprang forth … like some fierce lion that the whole countryside has met to hunt and kill – at first he bodes no ill, but when some daring youth has struck him with a spear, he crouches openmouthed, his jaws foam, he roars with fury, he lashes his tail from side to side about his ribs and loins, and glares as he springs straight before him, to find out whether he is to slay, or be slain among the foremost of his foes – even with such fury did Achilles burn.

Whatever changes mankind has undergone since then, one thing has remained constant, and that's man's ability to bear a grudge. A man's hurt pride has been the fuel for many a conflict: the Trojan war effectively started because someone stole someone else's wife; with the huge ensuing death toll this has to rank as one of the most costly infidelities of all time. In modern and much more benign times, men don't react quite so violently to such upsets; but there's still a nice parallel to be drawn between the rage of Achilles and the wrath of Steven Gerrard. As a schoolboy Gerrard had been rejected by the National School of Excellence at Lilleshall, and the resentment still ate at him when, some months later, Lilleshall's first team came to Melwood to play against Liverpool's academy side. It was the perfect opportunity for revenge, and as his autobiography records, he was more than ready to take it:

The first whistle made the same impression on me as a bell in a prize fight. A call to arms, the signal for battle. I smashed Lilleshall's midfield to pieces. Absolutely shredded them. Into every tackle I poured all my frustration at being wronged by the National School. I loved the thought of their coaches standing helplessly on the touchline as I tore into their chosen ones. 'This will show them what they rejected', I thought as I crunched another set of shin pads. 'This will make them see how wrong they were', I told myself as I sent another of their precious boys flying. 'Calm down', the ref kept shouting at me. No chance. Those Lilleshall boys were getting it big-time. Nothing was going to stop me. How could a referee understand my pain?

Maybe, in a different life, Thierry Henry might also have shared Achilles' violent intent; in this life it's fair to say that he, too, is driven by a savage internal fire. Whilst Ronaldinho's joyful appearance masks a darker agenda, Henry has been more honest about his motivations. A couple of days before Arsenal met Barcelona in the 2005 Champions League final, he admitted that 'that desire and that anger – in the right way – always drives me. People are scared of anger and that's one thing I always say about Rooney. You see it when he plays. That's what I mean when I talk about anger. I'm not scared of using my anger in a positive way. It's really difficult but without that anger I wouldn't be the same player … I want to have it in me until I stop.' Frequent viewers of Henry's goal celebrations would not be at all surprised by this confession. As often as not he doesn't smile upon scoring, but releases a wordless scream at some ecstatic section of the crowd. It's thus that in his moment of greatest euphoria, he seems at his most combustible; fittingly, his teammates leap on him as if they're blankets smothering a flame.

Henry's wrath, unlike that of Achilles, arises not through grief but through choice, and so there's no foe that he faces as formidable as himself. When he screams after scoring, it's likely that he's cursing whatever internal voice of doubt that he'd been arguing with before the match. A case in point was a goal that Henry scored against West Ham in the Premiership, a strike that seared through thirty yards of air before finding the top corner of David James' net. Arsenal had been trailing by two goals to nil when Henry lost his temper to spectacular effect. 'My goal was an anger strike', he'd later recall. 'I had so much anger at being two goals down. It was instinct because I was so fed up at that point.'

A bemused Vic Wakeling had noted these dark depths in Henry's apparently still waters. 'Every now and then, of course, people blur the line between passion and – as you've used the word, 'madness' – and it's over the top, it's out of control, they've flipped', he told me. 'Even Thierry Henry, who we all think is probably one of the most articulate, careful guys that's ever played in the English game, flipped when Arsenal scored the equaliser the other day.' The incident in question occurred in a Premiership match in early February 2007: following an own goal by the unfortunate Fitz Hall, Henry stood eye to eye with the Wigan goalkeeper Chris Kirkland, goading him. '[Seeing that] you suddenly think, "oh, crikey, we expect better of you." But, if that's his one slip that we all point to, you think: "well, hang on a second, how well controlled have you been the rest of the time?"'

Yet Henry's mastered the art of 'playing on the edge' better than most. This endless lust for a challenge is one that, as he remarked, he shared with Wayne Rooney, but it's one that the Scouser has found a little more difficult to channel. As Simon Barnes has written:

> Rooney is no precious ball player who finds opposition mildly dismaying: opposition is the wellspring of his footballing self. He likes people to drive at, to shrug off, to leave fallen, to leave confounded... This is not just a physical feat: it is also a mental one. Rooney doesn't play cold. He doesn't play in a serene, trance-like state. He is not the one cool head in the heat of battle. No: he *is* the heat of battle.

That heat is what all of the dominant athletes have within them; it's just that some make it more conspicuous than others. Barnes told me that when he met Sir Steve Redgrave, the five-times Olympic rowing gold medalist, it 'was like being introduced to a volcano'. Even Bjorn Borg, the Wimbledon champion from 1976 to 1980, who was stereotyped as the ice-cool Swede, had his inner inferno.

We've now dealt fully with the tempestuous forward, but there's an equal lack of sanity at the other end of the pitch. One of football's fondest and most enduring clichés is that goalkeepers are mad. Brian Glanville, the elder statesman of football writing, even wrote an entire novel – *Goalies are Different* – on that thesis. It's not a stereotype without foundation. The goalkeeper is the only player on the pitch with the privilege of controlling the ball with any part of his body; however, his power to use his hands is withdrawn as soon as he crosses a clearly marked boundary. He's also the only player on the pitch who's effectively confined to an area six yards across, and so unskilled are his feet relative to those of his teammates that he's unlikely to be effective further up the field at any rate.

What's more, the goalkeeper's in a position unlike anyone else in the stadium; he's at once spectator and participant in the action before him, forced to move between nervy inactivity and full engagement at a moment's notice. Far from the intensity of midfield battle, he must work harder than any of his teammates to immerse himself in the atmosphere of the match, and is more likely than any of the other players to be distracted by the cheers or curses that cascade from the stands. Bob Wilson, Arsenal's goalkeeper in their historic Double-winning season of 1971, has in his autobiography described this isolation better than most:

> The greatest appeal of the 'beautiful game' is to see a ball hit the rigging. For one player, however, that goalscoring moment signals failure, possible defeat, often humiliation, even despair. That is the goalkeeper's lot. He is a race apart, one of a breed who has to cope with the loneliness and the peculiarities of the job, its single-minded confrontational face, the vulnerability, the obligatory presence ...

When it's put like this, the case for goalkeepers being the strangest of a very strange bunch is almost overwhelming. But to play their position isn't a choice, it's a compulsion – or, more kindly, it's a calling. Peter Shilton, who remains England's most-capped player with 125 caps, has said that 'I think you're born a keeper. I always wanted to be the goalkeeper from the first moment someone put two coats down in the playground and said "who's going in goal?" Goalkeepers have to be a bit different in terms of personality and attitude. I think it's that mentality of not wanting to be beaten.'

Shilton's most memorable tormentor, by means both fair and foul, was of course Diego Maradona, who made clear his contempt for that part of the footballing profession. Of Shilton, he has written, 'The thermos-head got cross because of my hand-goal. What about the other one, Shilton, didn't you see that one? He didn't invite me to his testimonial … oh, my heart bleeds! How many people go to a goalkeeper's testimonial anyway? A goalkeeper's!'

No goalkeepers have managed to escape Maradona's wrath, regardless of their holiness. In fact, His Holiness Pope John Paul II felt the force of Diego's ire. As Maradona recounted, 'I fell out with the Pope. I went to the Vatican and I saw that the ceilings were made of gold. And I heard the Pope saying the church takes care of poor children, but if so, sell the ceiling, tiger. Do something! You've got nothing going for you. You were only a goalkeeper.'

Maradona's contempt may have been due in part to the comic nature of the role that the goalkeeper plays. Viewers of international football for much of the 1990s will be familiar with the work of Fabien Barthez, of Monaco, Manchester United and France, who provided both security and slapstick for his careworn defence. They'll also know the work of José Luis Chilavert, the Paraguay international who played for Racing Club Strasbourg and Vélez Sarsfield en route to the title of 1996 South American Footballer of the Year. Chilavert, and more recently Rogério Ceni of São Paulo, have reinterpreted the goalkeeper's role, playing almost as auxiliary attackers; both of them have achieved startling proficiency from free kicks and penalties, and occupy the top two places on the list of goalkeepers who've scored the most goals, with over sixty each at the time of writing.

But it's the player who occupies third place on this list who was so odd that he even won the affection of Maradona, showing that, whether or not you need madness to be great, it'll definitely help you to get into Diego's good books. René Higuita of Colombia had it in spades: Maradona described him as 'a beautiful character … a *loco*.' Higuita, who played 69 times for his national side, scoring three goals, is most famous for two equally iconic moments. The first of these was when he stopped a cross-shot from England's Jamie Redknapp at Wembley by leaping airborne and flipping his heels over his head (the 'scorpion kick'). The second, more calamitous, occasion came in the second round of the World Cup: he tried to dribble upfield and was caught in possession by Cameroon's Roger Milla, who then sped past him to put the Africans into the quarter-finals. Off the field, he served seven months for acting as the intermediary in the kidnapping of a drug lord's daughter. But Higuita's most significant achievement wasn't scoring dozens of goals, or even retaining the friendship of a man as capricious as Maradona; it was that, even though every vaguely eccentric footballer to have played in Spain or South America is nicknamed *El Loco*, Higuita was *the* original *El Loco*. Sure, there were, among others: Martin '*El Loco*' Palermo of Boca Juniors, Nourredine '*El Loco*' Naybet of Deportivo La Coruña, River Plate's René '*El Loco*' Houseman and Hugo '*El Loco*' Gatti (himself a goalkeeper) and Ramon (you've guessed it) '*El Loco*' Quiroga of (inevitably) Deportivo Wanka. But, due to the existence of Higuita, there was – as goes the old football chant – "only one *El Loco*".

With Higuita in mind, or rather whilst he was out of his, I wanted to find out more about goalkeepers and their mental processes; so I did something a little bizarre, which was therefore in keeping with the title of this chapter. The best goalkeeper that I'd encountered outside professional football was an American called Tyler Nottberg, who played between the posts for a rival college at university. Nottberg, a graduate student from Virginia who'd been doing a second degree in politics, philosophy and economics, had produced a save so brilliant in one of our games that it had stuck in my mind for years: it was the Sunday league equivalent of that denial of Pelé by Gordon Banks in the 1970 World

Cup. That was no exaggeration; when the ball had rolled free to our team's best finisher just seven yards from goal, half of our team were almost leaping in early celebration of the score. Our striker, Douthwaite, had taken no chances with this opening, and had powered a drive towards the bottom corner of the net, only for Nottberg, diving and jack-knifing into the path of the ball, to deflect it up and over the bar with the very tips of his fingers, the ball carrying so fast that it bounced only once before ending up on the river bank twenty yards away. Seeing that save as vividly as I did eight years later, I decided to contact Nottberg, since he, if anyone, would know about the strange things that went on in a top goalkeeper's mind.

He'd been more than personable on each of the five occasions when our paths had crossed on the football field, perhaps due to my failure to beat him during those seven hours, and we'd talked briefly about keeping in touch. We hadn't, and so when I wrote to him out of the blue almost a decade later, he didn't recall the save in question; either he'd made many of that nature over the years, or the experience had been more traumatic for me than it had been for him. I think at first he was bemused that I'd contacted him; then, reassured that I wasn't some dysfunctional striker who was bearing a lasting grudge, he was flattered. He'd done well for himself since leaving university. Having relocated to Kansas City, he was now the CEO of US Engineering, his family's company, and four weeks before I'd dropped him a line, he and his wife Leigh had had their second child, Andrew, who joined their three-year-old daughter Maggie. With all that on his plate, the last thing that he needed was more homework, but he kindly agreed to tackle the handful of pencil-chewing questions that I sent over to him. I wanted to know what he thought of Shilton's quote, that being a goalkeeper was not a matter of nature but one of nurture. He thought that was a fair comment:

Fundamentally, I would agree with the idea that one has to *want* to play goalkeeper. In that sense, goalkeepers *are* born. Great players would likely tell you that any position on the pitch has the potential to this claim, though. Forwards might say that you have to be born a forward because you have to have a nose for the goal ... After I saved my first shot, I realised immediately that everything about that position fit who I am. Footballers don't so much learn a position as they find one.

Nottberg's favourite goalkeeper was the Denmark international Peter Schmeichel, a man who aimed to impose his will on his opponents. Schmeichel seemed to play football a little like basketball players might contest a game of one-on-one, making goalkeeping a form of personal confrontation. But Nottberg pointed out that goalkeepers were most likely oblivious to the personalities whom they were facing, their attention focused on a more important matter. 'The only personal contest was between me and the ball', he confessed. 'I never cared whether it was a defender who'd come up for a shot, a striker, or a midfielder. I had good rivalries with friends on opposing teams, but I rarely thought about them when I was playing. It was always the ball that mattered the most.'

Nottberg's footballing existence was even more hermetic than I'd suspected. Not only did goalkeepers spend large sections of the game uninvolved in play, they also tended to disregard the presence of their peers on the pitch. I'd also wondered whether, with all of the pressure and isolation that comes with being a goalkeeper, it was a fair description to say that goalkeepers were a little bit crazy. I was slightly worried about eliciting a partisan and defensive response, which is why I didn't address him in my e-mail as Tyler *'El Loco'* Nottberg, but my concerns proved baseless. Nottberg went on to write:

Joe Machnik, who was a goalkeeper coach for the US National Team, once told me while I was attending his camp that goalkeepers have to be 'mad'. In the UK, 'mad' means crazy. In the States, 'mad' generally means angry. I think it is a bit of both. Goalkeepers who are the most eccentric get a lot of press and are labelled 'crazy'. But the survivors like Shilton, Schmeichel, Barthez, [Sepp] Maier, and [Oliver] Kahn are closer to the US meaning – angry. I always felt angry when I played – angry at the opposing team, angry at my own team, angry when I stopped a shot, angry if I let in a shot. Generally, nobody likes you during the game, but they respect you, and your teammates believe in you when you call for the ball on a cross.

His words could have been written by Thierry Henry. They echoed much of what Vic Wakeling had said about him losing his temper in the light of the Wigan game, and suggested that goalkeepers were indeed the misanthropic race that I'd suspected them to be, albeit that they weren't alone in this respect. Why all that anger, I wondered. Nottberg's answer was a simple one: 'Anger is ... the antidote to fear – fear of failure and fear of getting hurt.' Maybe that was the crux of it – whether you were Steven Gerrard, Thierry Henry or '*El Loco*' Nottberg, you had to erect a barrier of passion against the equally passionate expectations of your colleagues and spectators. Walling yourself in like that sounded like a lonely business. You'd think it would make sense to let some of that out, so that you wouldn't feel so isolated; but when Zidane did so via that head–butt, and was dismissed for his trouble, he ended up lonelier than ever.

It just goes to show that you can't please football fans; they want to see passion, to reassure them that this player, whom they've paid to see, cares about their cause. They want him to make a proud and outward show of his hunger, but they – we – don't realise that, for some players, passion isn't something that you allow to seep out through your pores just so that you can impress people. It's highly combustible stuff, and, as a result, is best kept under wraps, and we shouldn't ask to see it. Because if we, like Marco Materazzi, continue to do so, we'll find that this madness makes players like Zidane wear their hearts not on their sleeves, but on their foreheads.

Aura

Some players are one-man swarms, their presence on the pitch over-whelming and relentless, surging through midfield with a feral intensity. Ruud Gullit, in the colours of AC Milan, PSV and Holland, was one such: so energetic, so charismatic, that he enchanted even those sent out to kick him. There's a famous story, possibly mythical, of an opponent looking over at him in the tunnel before a match and shaking. Simon Kuper told me of the time before the 1998 European Championship final against Germany, when Gullit walked out to inspect the pitch and went to speak with a German player whom he knew; many of the other German players 'just stood around, gazing up at him'. As Simon Garfield noted in *The Observer*, 'You could tell who the other players on the pitch thought was the greatest among them by the determined rush for Gullit's shirt at the end of the match.'

Other players aren't like this: they move across the pitch with a rare, faintly ominous menace, and, like snipers, announcing themselves only once they have struck. Into this bracket of silent-thus-deadly falls Raúl Gonzalez Blanco of Real Madrid and Spain, who by the age of 24 was already the greatest player in his nation's history. By then, he'd acquired two Primera Liga titles, and become the top scorer in the UEFA Champions League, on the way to no less than three European Cups. He replaced a similarly predatory striker, Emilio Butragueño, who was himself known as 'The Vulture' in the Madrid first team, and promptly cast a foreboding spell over Continental football. He was not a spectacular player, nor notably fast; but in the first seven years of his career, Raúl accumulated goals at the rate of one every two games, with the same sense of entitlement as a taxman coming to collect his due. In an era where even superstars such as Luis Figo were available at the right price, it was declared that Raúl was not for sale; indeed, he seemed on his way to the greatest career ever seen in the modern game. Then, for whatever reason, Raúl lost it.

All of the best footballers – in fact, all of the best athletes – have it: Tiger Woods, approaching the eighteenth hole of the final round in a major tournament; Pete Sampras, in a fourth-set tiebreak on Centre Court at Wimbledon; Michael Jordan at the free-throw line in the dying seconds of the NBA Finals; Roy Keane in the tunnel, five minutes before kick-off. It's that look: deceptively faraway but intensely, almost violently focused on the here and now. It's also that presence, the square-shouldered stance in the face of fate or the swagger towards destiny. In sum, it's an aura, a quality that creates a sense of reverence whenever the athlete approaches, both on and off the field of play. To illustrate this theme, I looked for a footballer who, even years after his retirement, would inspire awe in those who met him. I found him, and met him, but I did so with absolutely no help from Pelé.

One of the most bizarre sporting documents of this or any other century is Pelé's list, commissioned by FIFA, of the 100 greatest living footballers. Not only does the list actually feature 125 names – among them, such classy but not all-conquering individuals as Robert Pirès and Javier Saviola – but it also has several shameful omissions: such as 'The King', Denis Law, of Manchester United and Scotland; like Pep Guardiola, for a decade the soul of Barcelona's midfield; like Dejan Savićević and Dragan Stojković, who for AC Milan, Red Star Belgrade and Yugoslavia, gave the world's defenders years of insomnia; and like Majid Abdullah.

A fair selection of you will have made a discreet double-take at that last name. If – as is likely – you were one of those neck-jerkers, then Majid Abdullah is the greatest footballer that you've never heard of. Born in Jeddah, Saudi Arabia, in 1958, and retiring after two decades at the top of the game in the Middle East, this brilliant left-footed striker is widely regarded as the finest that the Asian region has ever produced. The bare statistics testify to this: he scored over five hundred goals, took his national side to the Olympics and the World Cup for the first time in its history, and played over one-hundred-and-fifty times in the colours of Saudi Arabia. He also had an impressive list of victims; in international matches, he scored against Scotland, England, Argentina and Brazil, and it was as a result of such feats that he was nicknamed 'the Desert Pelé'. This, however, was insufficient to stop the South American Pelé from overlooking him, or from revealing only a few hundred hits when his name was keyed into any reputable internet search engine.

In fact, it was markedly easier to contact Majid Abdullah in the flesh than it was to find him online; perhaps, I considered, this was as elusive as he had been on the pitch during his playing days. When I consulted www.google.com, I found that this footballer was almost outshone by his namesake, Abdul Majid Abdullah, who was one of the most well-loved singers in the Arab world. Like the footballer, this musician's gifts had gone largely unnoticed beyond the continent of his birth.

I'd heard of Majid Abdullah but wasn't sure where, in the same way that I didn't quite remember when I had first heard the initials JFK; knowledge of both of these distant figures had permeated my consciousness many years ago, even though I had hardly seen footage of either in action. There was a curious gap between Majid Abdullah's iconic status on his continent, where he had regularly played in front of crowds that would dwarf those of Saturdays at Old Trafford, and his virtual invisibility in Western media, a state of affairs that perhaps displayed the lack of respect still shown to the Arab game. But somehow his fame had transcended these prejudices, to the extent that FC Barcelona had invited him to their city as a special guest of theirs.

How do you prepare to meet a living legend? How would he behave when I met him? What kind of aura would he have? These were the questions that I asked myself as I awaited my flight to the Spanish coast. Some footballers, such as Johann Cruyff and Eric Cantona, wilfully wove veils of such mystery about themselves, cloaking themselves carefully in so much vanity, that for a moment you believed that they were gods and not men. Cantona, in particular, became infamous for trying to pass off the most banal of comments as the most cutting-edge pieces of philosophy. However, he was occasionally capable of statements of arresting beauty. It's a widely-accepted fact that many players have trouble coming to terms with the end of their professional careers, and are faced with the dilemma of what they should do next. That's how a mere mortal would describe the situation – not Cantona. He pronounced that 'often there are players who have only football as a way of expressing themselves and never develop other interests. And when they no longer play football, they no longer do anything; they no longer exist, or rather they have the sensation of no longer existing.'

Would Majid Abdullah be the same way, diminished by a life after football and away from the grand stage? Hunter Davies implicitly acknowledged the terrible feeling of emasculation that occurs when the most defining platform of your life is taken from you. He observed in the *New Statesman* that 'Roy Keane himself was in the studio, and being handled with caution and reverence. He still has his aura, which not all star players retain once their career is over. Bobby Moore and Bobby Charlton became mere mortals when they retired. Keano might no longer give you a kicking, but he could still manage a tongue-lashing.'

Another player who was similarly content having hung up his boots was John Collins; this acclaimed defensive midfielder had gone from Celtic, then to AS Monaco, Fulham and Everton, picking up almost sixty Scotland caps along the way. As I spoke to him by telephone to Monte Carlo, the summer before he was due to take over as manager of Hibernian, he was happy and relaxed, having put the finishing touches on his UEFA coaching qualifications. In the course of the interview, I gained a sense of how difficult it must have been for some footballers to leave the limelight. As Collins noted, 'If you look at all the top players, they thrive on the big crowds.' It sounded like an addictive feeling, but one off which he seemed to have weaned himself quite easily. He spoke with nostalgia and admiration of many of his former teammates, with whom he had won the French championship in 1996. They had numbered such luminaries as the Belgian genius Enzo Scifo, Brazil's Sonny Anderson, Emmanuel Petit and Fabien Barthez, as well as the young David Trezeguet and Thierry Henry. Interestingly, and above all of these, he reserved a special word for Ali Benarbia, who in England would be best known to Manchester City followers. He believed that Benarbia had never got the recognition that he deserved, and that had a certain Zinedine Zidane not existed, he'd have been the France number-ten for many years. With Collins keen to share his ideas about the modern game, ours was a fluent discussion; notably, the only time that it slowed in pace was when I asked him the name of the best opponent he'd ever faced. 'Zidane', he said. 'He was a complete artist, he was like a dancer with the ball. If you watch closely, most players have got only one move [that they can use to beat a defender]. Very few players have three or four moves, like Zidane did.'

He was similarly impressed by Frank Rijkaard's work as Barcelona's manager. As a former neighbour of Rijkaard's, he had been invited to the Nou Camp to watch the first team training behind closed doors, and came away enthused by the 'calm and happy sessions' that he had seen. Despite the terrific pressure that Barça were under at that time, riding high in the league and in thrilling pursuit of the UEFA Champions League, they were a side very much at ease; and that was thanks to Rijkaard's influence. 'Often', noted Collins, 'a team reflects a manager's personality'. Moreover, when I mentioned that I was going to speak with Majid Abdullah, he was intrigued, seemingly more knowledgeable about the man than many European journalists – myself included.

Nervous as I already was about this meeting, my concern was only deepened after the somewhat terse conversation that I had with Majid Abdullah as soon as I landed in Barcelona. He sounded surprised to hear from me, and then asked me if I could interview him at 10 p.m. that night, or possibly the next day. Given that my flight home was scheduled for 9 p.m., his initial suggestion fell on crestfallen ears. Thankfully, he rearranged his plans, and agreed to meet me at the Arts Hotel in Barcelona at 5 p.m., where he'd give me twenty minutes of his time.

I was taken aback by this; I'd complacently assumed that I would be able to have an hour-long audience, but such was the congestion of his diary that I feared I wouldn't be able to gain sufficient material in that time. Still, I thought, looking on the bright side, at least he hadn't been as tough to pin down as Nwankwo Kanu. I'd tried to arrange an interview with the former Inter, Arsenal and Ajax star, in the summer after the 2006 World Cup; on two occasions I'd confirmed the date of an interview with him, once in the Midlands and once in north London, only for him to disappear without a trace as soon as the fateful day arrived. He became impossible to contact, and my growing fears for his safety were eased only when he resurfaced on Match of the Day in the colours of Portsmouth FC, apparently in the form of his life as he fired them to the top of the Premiership table. Whether his resurgent form was caused by the bracing seaside air, or by his euphoria at having escaped from my queries about the game, I really don't know.

But back to Majid. As I made my way across the town, first via the bus and then via the clammy underground system, I thought of the only other footballer whom I had met to date: Edgar Davids, the ebullient Dutch midfielder who'd jealously guarded possession of the ball for Ajax, Juventus, both Milans, Barcelona and, latterly, Tottenham. This had been a chance encounter at the Notting Hill Carnival, the day after Davids had played for Juventus against Milan in the Italian Supercup. The game had ended in a 2–2 draw; Davids had been extraordinary, a performance befitting his then status as one of the finest two or three defensive midfielders in the world. As I approached him in a cluttered side street near Westbourne Park tube station, he bore little resemblance to the man who'd been proudly patrolling the centre-circle with Zidane just the day before. There was one tell-tale sign of his superstardom – he was accompanied by a tall icicle of a brunette, who seemed to have swanned straight from a world-class catwalk – but otherwise his body language was hunched and apologetic, almost timid. This was under-whelming. I couldn't believe how short he was, and how narrow were his shoulders; it was as if he'd shrunk the moment he had left the pitch. Oddly, it left me with even more respect for him, that someone so diminutive could acquit himself physically to such compelling effect. I'd mumbled something to him about being a very big fan of his, almost requested an autograph, and then – remembering that I was eighteen – retreated in a state of barely-veiled embarrassment.

But the Davids meeting had reinforced my view that only the greatest players have that special atmosphere around them at all times. In that street, he'd been as wide-eyed as any other passer-by, whereas had I come across, say, Ruud Gullit, I'd have surely cut him a wide and respectful berth. And prominent athletes often love to project this air of supremacy, knowing, as did Raphael Burke, that the primary battle in sport is psychological. Michael Jordan, in a documentary about his career, candidly described his state of mind when he was at his peak. 'The feeling is you own the ball', he shrugged. 'You own the game, you own the guy who is guarding you – you can actually play him like a puppet.' Jordan saw the game as some form of predetermined drama, ending in his inevitable victory; he'd already seen success in his mind's eye, and the player guarding him was merely a member of the supporting cast, blindly acting out a confirmation of Jordan's greatness. And so an aura is a strangely hypnotic thing: it entrances the opposition, entraps them into thinking, although the match may not even have begun, that they've already lost.

With the huge advantage that an aura can confer, there are several teams who've worked consciously to maintain one. Chief among these is Real Madrid, of whom Phil Ball has written that 'the club embodies the Spanish sporting concept of *Machacar* (crush without mercy) ... You don't let your opponents off the hook, and you rarely allow the bull to live. There's no poetry in that.' A reason for Madrid's longevity at the top of the game could be that they have married this savage streak with a pristine strip that gives them a deceptive innocence: how could a team dressed so divinely cause such terrible damage? Phil Ball continued: 'It is the pure simplicity of Real Madrid's all-white that begins to catch the eye. It is not so much a case of their playing any better as yet, but rather the strange threat that resides in the quiet dignity of their colours, as if the conscious decision to keep it plain has been based on some sort of inner confidence.'

Or based, perhaps, on a desire to hide the wolf within. As discussed earlier, no one's quite sure if Zidane was an angel or demon; the same contradiction exists in the personality of Real Madrid. Maybe Zidane

157

embodied their ethos better than he himself even realised. But it was another Madrid player who considered Zidane to be the player who was the most in his own likeness – indeed, he referred to him as 'maestro' – and who came in for particular praise when I spoke to Hugh McIlvanney. 'If you're talking about aura, then the greatest example of aura that I have ever witnessed was di Stefano', he said. 'Jesus Christ! ... You know, he was playing with the best players in the world, and [on the pitch] he was telling them "go here, go there" ... on the park, I don't think there's ever been anyone who could hold a candle to him in terms of sheer presence. He was a monster.'

Madrid's aura – elegant, therefore deadly – has seduced an endless line of the world's finest talents to further their careers at the Santiago Bernabéu. Liverpool's men, clad in imperial crimson, once swept all before them, and though the Anfield club has gone through a period of relative decline it retains its extraordinary presence. It's probable that the very act of playing for Liverpool has falsely intimidated opposing teams into thinking that a player was better than he actually was. The Brazilian shirt is another case in point. Since the glorious anointment of their predecessors at the 1970 World Cup, several Brazilian players have used the famous yellow shirt as a mask for their relative mediocrity. For example, Ze Roberto, a left-winger, was employed as a defensive midfielder at the 2006 World Cup, a role which was akin to expecting Ryan Giggs to do the job of Claude Makalélé. Yet in Brazil's opening match of that tournament, a bland 1–0 victory, the Croatians failed to force the initiative in midfield, as if expecting Ze Roberto to perform with the grit and gravitas that Dunga had shown in years gone by.

Contests down the ages, whether sporting or military, have relied on pre-match hype. Julius Caesar may have been defeated on his first visit to England partly because its inhabitants had no form guide, and their minds weren't burdened by the weight of the Roman legend. In recent years, Brazil have been both the masters and the victims of pre-match hype: Nike, their main sponsors, have been too successful in creating an air of expectation around them, one which has apparently bred a sense of complacency and *fait accompli* in the players themselves. Before the

2006 World Cup, the slogan *Joga Bonito* – the exhortation to 'play beautifully' – appeared everywhere except, apart from a few titillating flashes, in the performances of Brazil. Somewhat defensively, Roberto Carlos dismissed any suggestion that they had bought into the frenzy whipped up by their sponsors. 'The *Joga Bonito* slogan was invented by a sports brand', he insisted. 'Don't blame us for that. Brazilian soccer is intelligent and winning, with great champions, and that's what we have always been. When you start talking about the beautiful game, that's more about selling things.' But, to paraphrase Shakespeare, methinks that the left-back doth protest too much. Roberto Carlos knew as well as anyone that Brazil had talked the talk prior to the tournament, but hadn't brought their walk with them.

Like Brazil, Majid Abdullah had also played in yellow in the prime years of his club career; it might make you wonder whether the colours that certain teams wear are a kind of brand of dominance, some subliminal signal that they sit atop the sporting kingdom. Russell A. Hill and Robert A. Barton, two evolutionary anthropologists at the University of Durham, have explored the success of athletes who wear the colour red, reasoning that colour has elsewhere played a large part in the hierarchies that exist in nature. Their paper, published in the science journal *Nature* in 2005, recorded the outcome of four combat sports at the 2004 Olympic Games – boxing, tae kwon do, Greco–Roman wrestling and freestyle wrestling – where contestants were randomly assigned either red or blue shirts. Assuming that most competitors at this level were fairly evenly matched, then the number of winners who wore red should not have been much different from the number of winners who wore blue. However, they found that 'for all four competitions, there is a consistent and statistically significant pattern in which contestants wearing red win more fights'; reds triumphed in 242 out of 441 bouts; moreover, red-shirted competitors triumphed in 62 per cent of close encounters. Hill and Barton went on to note that 'although other colours are also present in animal displays, it is specifically the presence and intensity of red coloration that correlates with male dominance and testosterone levels. In humans, anger is associated with a reddening of the skin due to increased blood flow, whereas fear is associated with increased pallor in similarly threatening situations. Hence, increased redness during aggressive interactions may reflect relative dominance.'

If we assume the status of football as a combat sport – a description at which many of those nostalgic for football's harder past may laugh – then this research seems partially to explain the primacy of red-shirted teams such as Liverpool, Arsenal and Manchester United, not, of course, to forget Michael Jordan's Chicago Bulls, or England's own World Cup-winning side of 1966. It's not so conclusive, however, given the place of Real Madrid in football's firmament; their shirt is the shade of 'increased pallor ... in threatening situations'.

More recently, two Germans have analysed the effect of shirt colour in the context of team sports. Matthias Sutter and Martin G. Kocher, from the economics departments of Cologne and Innsbruck universities, considered the results of the 2000–1 Bundesliga season; they did so in the light of Hill's and Barton's findings, which some felt suggested that if Germany chose a red shirt for the 2006 World Cup it would give them a slight edge. Yet they discovered that 'the colour of the teams' shirts does not have any significant influence on the outcome of a match. One explanation for the discrepancy between individual combat sports and team sports with regard to the effects of colour on performance is that the effects of colour are supposed to be much less salient in a team because other factors like team cohesion or the support by teammates are more dominant.'

In the end, any aura that was created by red shirts was of minimal effect; in a tournament whose final stages were marked by tight games and a virtual absence of goals, there were no red-shirted teams in the final. Portugal, in maroon, succumbed to France at the semi-final stage; Spain, the World Cup's last survivors in red, were dispatched by Zidane in the second round. But, as Barton dryly noted, 'If you're rubbish, a red shirt won't stop you from losing.'

So shirt colour's an irrelevance; but a good captain is not. I received several similar e-mails on this topic, the most typical being that of Ozan Ozkural, who wrote that 'leadership is a very important quality that should be included. That is, a player's ability to generate trust from teammates, and the ability to act as a coach in the field'. Simon Barnes, writing shortly after the 2006 World Cup, didn't just think it very important: he thought it the criterion that separated a very, very good player from an indisputably great one. He set out his theory thus in *The Times*:

> When it comes to football, at least, I think I have the answer. Scan a player for possible greatness and ask: does he score goals? Good. Does he make goals? Good again. But now for the question that actually matters: does he make teams? Has he created a great international team in his own image, by the brilliance of his play and the force of his mind?

By that token, he nominated Zidane to join the small and proud elite of Maradona, Pelé, Beckenbauer and Cruyff. His reasoning was simple. 'Martin Johnson, the England rugby union captain in the World Cup triumph of 2003, said that he never set himself up to be a leader', wrote Barnes. 'It was just that people tended to follow him, demonstrating that the true gift of leadership is the ability to inspire "followship" in everyone else. That was always something that Zidane was able to do.'

I felt that leadership was a category that fell within the general sphere of aura, since many great footballers have inspired their colleagues as much by their presence as with their words, but Ozkural's point made me ask myself who the game's finest leader might have been. Naturally, there were several fierce competitors for such a title, not least England's Tony Adams and Bobby Moore, Spain's Fernando Hierro and Manuel Sanchis; but, all things considered, I had to side with the German who, in the words of tennis star Boris Becker, was 'nicknamed the "Kaiser" for his dominating yet distinguished style of play'.

Franz Beckenbauer, or 'the Emperor', won the World Cup in 1974, the European Championship in 1972, three European Cups with Bayern Munich between 1974 and 1976, was twice voted European Footballer of the Year (in 1972 and 1976), and – as Becker reminds us in *Time*

Europe magazine – 'became the first man to take home the World Cup both as captain in 1974 and as manager when he coached the last West German team to victory in 1990'. But those are just statistics. As Henry Kissinger – again moonlighting as a sportswriter – has put it, 'It is not just for the medals and trophies that Beckenbauer is remembered. Rather it is for the style and the genius. Every movement he made on the pitch bristled with elegance.'

Beckenbauer's position was that of attacking sweeper, a role both conservative and aggressive, forming both the last line of defence and the first line of attack. As well as being of much tactical danger to the opposition – Beckenbauer's arrival late and from deep was troubling to the most sophisticated defences – it was also a useful psychological tool; it meant that Beckenbauer was influential anywhere on the pitch, either in halting their approaches or launching many of his own.

If, then, to have an aura is to own the space around you, then the best examples of this quality must be defenders and goalkeepers, players who guard their ground with often ferocious resolve. Of course, Italy has produced an endless line of sweepers and fullbacks who have made their goals seem as secure as any gated community. Among these, Paolo Maldini stands out, the man who made his debut for AC Milan at sixteen and was still dominant in the same shirt twenty years later. He was not one of those defenders whose feet treat the ball like a newly-unpinned grenade and therefore launch it as far from themselves as possible with all available haste. His rare gift was to be unhurried, yet never casual, regardless of the calibre of striker that he was facing, a platform upon which his team built four European Cup victories and several more Serie A titles. Many supporters will have their favourite Maldini moment, and this is mine: on one occasion in Serie A, one of Verona's forwards had tried to outfox Maldini by scooping the ball over his head, then running around him to collect it on the other side. Maldini had watched the ball float above him, then spun upon the axis of his right heel and pulled the ball down with the outside of his left foot, before passing it calmly infield to one of his centre-backs. The San Siro crowd gasped in approval; the forward was presumably tempted to do the same.

The Maldini slide tackle was as aesthetically perfect as any one of Cruyff's turns or Beckham's free kicks, its controlled violence a surprise from a man of such elegance that he even modelled for Armani. When Maldini tackled a player in this way it was not only an act of dispossession, but also a statement of intent; tall but not thin, serene yet swift, he'd swing his front leg into the path of the oncoming attacker, scooping the ball up and away from danger and leaving the striker with a pair of whiplashed ankles. In the process, he often seemed to engulf opponents, so conclusive was the nature of this contact. Sjaak Swart, who played for Ajax in the golden days of the 1970s, once commented of his team's dominance that 'when we played in our own stadium, teams who came here were afraid of us. In the bus they were already trembling. Many old players have told me this. Before the game started, it was already 1–0 to us.' It may be that teams coming to play AC Milan in Maldini's heyday were similarly afraid of the prospect of going a goal behind, given the difficulty that they'd then have of breaching the home team's rearguard with this defender at the helm.

But brilliant though he was, Maldini wasn't alone in making his defence a no-fly zone for strikers. He was partnered in crime by Franco Baresi, who was, alongside Franz Beckenbauer, one of the two finest sweepers that the world has known. With Maldini and Baresi working in tandem, approaching their goal was often a dispiriting process, never evidenced more than in the 1993–4 Serie A season. That year, AC Milan won the league championship despite scoring only 36 times in 34 games – a record low total for champions in the modern era, and one (thankfully) that is unlikely to be lowered. That they still won the league was due to their extraordinary defensive record, which saw them concede only fifteen goals. Baresi was, like Maldini, a *bandiera* – a player, like Raúl Gonzalez in his early years at Real Madrid, who epitomises the club's finest values – but his methods were somewhat more cunning. He had the subtle skill of getting away with fouls in plain sight of the referee, tugging and nudging to force forwards away from their centres of gravity. Accordingly, the enduring memories of him are at a stoppage in play, cupping his hands and pleading his case to a match official with all the passion and persistence of a trained barrister.

If we're talking, though, of the ability of a player to intimidate opponents at the closest quarters, then we can't fail to mention the goalkeeper. Since he generally receives fewer touches of the ball during a game than most other footballers, the presence that he transmits is his most important asset. At his worst, he's a scrambling and hapless soul, the man upon whom all focus falls in the event of a narrow defeat. At his best, he treats the penalty area like some expensive freehold that he's recently and proudly acquired, bellowing at teammates and opposition alike in case they should spend too long on his estate. In other words, he's Peter Schmeichel, perhaps the best goalkeeper ever and certainly the most territorial. Schmeichel, whose career included eight extraordinary years at Manchester United and a record-breaking tenure as Denmark's goalkeeper – some 129 caps – managed to keep one clean sheet almost every two games, an outstanding record. Though he was gifted with fine reflexes, athleticism, and a huge frame – he wore an XXXL jersey and was six-foot-four – his most significant attribute was that he made his goalmouth an inhospitable place to visit. There were many times when he seemed to have as much contempt for his back four as he had for Michael Owen, Luis Figo or whichever forward he was in the course of frustrating, with his right-back Gary Neville more often than not the object of his scorn.

There can't have been many sportsmen, let alone footballers, more bullish than Peter Schmeichel in his prime. He could hurl the ball to the halfway line, and early in his Manchester United career, against Tottenham, he punted it almost into the other goalkeeper's six-yard box. While he was therefore capable of huge physical influence on a match's outcome, he was also able to pull off saves that were demoralising in their quality. The one that springs most immediately to mind is the one he made against Ivan Zamorano of Internazionale in the first leg of the 1999 UEFA Champions League quarter-final. Manchester United led 2–0 at Old Trafford, and it was midway through the second half. Zamorano, known in his Real Madrid days as 'The Helicopter' due to his ability seemingly to hover in the air whilst heading the ball, flung his forehead at a high, looping cross from the left wing; from six yards out, he made perfect contact, and the ball seared towards the bottom right-hand corner of the net. But then Schmeichel, with an upward flap of his left arm that was as quick as a hummingbird's wing, somehow swatted the ball clear for a corner. Zamorano, crestfallen, failed to score in either leg of the tie; Internazionale, perhaps inevitably, lost.

This Chilean wasn't the sole forward to have cause to curse Schmeichel over the years. In a game that effectively sealed the destination of the 1996–7 Premier League title, Newcastle's Les Ferdinand saw him deflect a drive of cruise-missile velocity over the crossbar. Bergkamp's penalty was repelled by him in the last minute of normal time of the 1999 FA Cup semi-final. Even the great Marco van Basten was humbled at the Dane's hands, having his attempt saved in a shootout during Denmark's remarkable run to the 1992 European Championship. Indeed, the only player who can claim to have made Schmeichel look merely human is Rivaldo, who in the space of a few months in 1998 – first in the colours of Brazil at the World Cup, and then twice for Barcelona in the UEFA Champions League – put the ball in his net no less than five times, with an array of chips, free kicks and low, raking strikes from distance.

Could Majid Abdullah, the man whose aura I was about to discover, have tamed Schmeichel? Maybe. There was a goal that he'd scored against China in the final of the 1988 Asian Nations Cup, the clinching strike in a 2-0 triumph for the Saudis. On a mud-ridden surface uneven as a cobbled path, he'd surged in from the left flank, leaving one defender transfixed, then a second, as he entered the area; and, finally, inexplicably, the goalkeeper fell flat on his backside, looking forlornly on as Abdullah arrowed past him and placed the ball inside his near post. It's only when I'd watched the replay that the reason for the goalkeeper's flailing tumble became clear: it wasn't the slippery pitch or the custodian's poor technique, but the shoulder-fake that he'd been sold, Abdullah drawing the ball into, then away from, his clutches as disdainfully as a matador's cloth.

It would take that kind of alpha-male arrogance to disarm the world's greatest defences, and I wanted to know if Majid Abdullah had it in person, if his on-pitch swagger would be reproduced in the artificial cool of a Spanish hotel foyer. I was certain by now that to overcome an ego as overbearing as that of Peter Schmeichel, a larger ego was needed, and maybe that's what Majid Abdullah had. After all, the top attackers needed that; when facing custodians of the ilk of Shilton, Zenga and Zoff, flamboyant self-belief was almost as important as a sound first touch. But as soon as I formed that thesis, I thought of Paul Scholes.

Roy Keane describes Scholes in his autobiography as 'arguably the most gifted player in our squad ... Paul was the perfect pro. Superb on the field, modest and sensible off it. No celebrity bullshit, no self-promotion or glory-hunting, an amazingly gifted player who remained an unaffected human being.' Paul Scholes threatened to be a one-man rebuttal of my theory that all great players have an aura. Six Premier League titles, half as many FA Cups, a UEFA Champions League medal, an impressive collection of decisive goals – often away from home – and not a hint of hubris. He differed from Raúl in that he wasn't marked out by a coldness or a contempt. The first time that I saw Paul Scholes play for Manchester United, he looked like a shy but naughty schoolboy, bashful to your face, but ready to bean you with a conker as soon as you weren't looking. He must take a great proportion of the credit for Manchester United's Treble triumph of 1999; whilst opposing teams were briefed almost to the point of boredom about the dangers posed by Beckham, Keane and Giggs, they never seemed mindful of the late, late runs from midfield that Scholes would make whenever the game was at its tightest. It was as if his game relied on the lack of aura, on its very opposite: a curious invisibility, making his presence known on the pitch only when he chose. Since, however, he was a unique player – no other footballer I knew could be so devastating yet so unobtrusive in the same moment – I decided to nominate him as the exception to my rule. As long as, that was, Majid Abdullah didn't turn out to be like Paul Scholes.

With such contradictions in mind I came, then, to the Arts Hotel, where three members of the Saudi striker's entourage were waiting in the lounge. After a few moments of small talk, in he came, and as I turned to meet him I was immediately struck by one thing: he looked just like your favourite uncle. He was a man of immense scale, with hands that could comfortably glove my own, and he stood two clear inches taller than me, despite the fact that I was myself over six feet in height. Yet he didn't cut an intimidating figure; he had soft hands and warm eyes, with long, firm arms that you could imagine two or three young nieces and nephews swinging from at any one time. He looked much younger than his forty-eight years of age, and healthy enough to be still involved in competitive sport at a decent level.

As we greeted each other, I quickly learned the reason for his abrupt tone during our telephone call; he was much more comfortable in Arabic than in English. He handed the translation duties to one of his companions, who was one of his oldest and closest friends, but despite that connection, he was clearly in awe of him. Acting as his translator, he insisted that I refer to Majid Abdullah as 'Mr Majid Abdullah' as the preface to each question, which was a few syllables too many to contend with as the interview clock ran down. Once we began talking, though, I saw that Majid Abdullah was someone who, refreshingly, understood and appreciated his role as a national icon. It turned out that in Saudi Arabia, they were even more obsessed with the game than they were in England, with, by his estimate, 'ninety to ninety-five per cent' of the country being football fans. It was the national sport, with no worthy competitors for that title. I explained my list of the eleven characteristics that made a great footballer, and he listened patiently; too patiently, I thought at first, and felt that I hadn't conveyed my point. But then he made clear that being a great footballer wasn't something that you could take for granted after you had quit the game. You had to work hard to maintain your reputation. 'Look at Maradona. He's no longer a great player', he said, almost as a lament. 'Look at the way he lives now, you don't see Pelé doing that.' Pelé occupied a special place in his heart. Though he had omitted Majid Abdullah from his list of Greatest Living Footballers, the Brazilian was the player that he admired most of all, and whom he still considered to be the finest ever.

In fact, at the only time during the interview when Abdullah's behaviour hinted that he'd been a footballing phenomenon – that hinted at the sheer force of will that had taken him to the top of the game – he became briefly, strongly reminiscent of Pelé. Though a softly-spoken interviewee, Abdullah's relaxed pose became a small explosion of movement when I asked him what was his favourite move for going past a defender. He jerked one arm up, then the other, thrusting his head aggressively side to side, miming for several seconds before speaking, but miming so effectively that by the time the translation came I didn't need it. 'I didn't have a favourite move', he said. 'My favourite move was whatever could beat the defender. I would go past him with my left foot, with my right foot, I would nod it past him, it didn't matter. Whatever it would take to beat him.' Like Pelé, he had been capable of instant control of the ball with almost any part of his body, and he told me that in his youth he had learned to play in all of the outfield positions and in goal, so that he could understand how everyone on the pitch was thinking. I asked him about his favourite goal from his long career, and his response – given his reaction to my query about his favourite move – was punchy and predictable. His accompanying grin was as wide, and cheeky, as any of Ronaldinho's. 'I have scored many goals', he said, 'and they are all my children! To ask me to tell you my favourite goal is to ask a proud father to tell you who is his favourite son.'

Phil Ball has commented that 'Raúl was once a great player, and may be again', that Raúl's status in that pantheon had been tarnished by three poor seasons in succession. The harsh truth was that Raúl had lost the aura which made him the point of reference whenever a match hung in the balance. This, however, shouldn't be seen as a casual dismissal of Raúl's legend; as we'll see later in this book, vision is a gift as mysterious and elusive as aura, even – and perhaps especially – to those who possess it. Majid Abdullah's scathing assessment of Maradona's troubled retirement made it clear that the mantle of greatness is not one lightly worn; Phil Ball's view of Raúl showed that it may be one easily surrendered. Perhaps the greatest example of an aura, though, came from Majid Abdullah, in an act of deep humility that could come only from someone who has been truly dominant in his art. The act came as he reached into his wallet at the end of my interview with him, as he took out a card which gave him membership of a prestigious FIFA committee. 'All of them are members of this committee', he said, himself awestruck, reeling off each famous name as a proud one-word sentence. 'Beckenbauer. Eusebio. Pelé.' Then, cradling his membership card like a piece of precious crystal, he pointed gently at his picture. 'And me', he beamed.

Luck

The most famous 'goal that never was' in English football history?

Many of you will know it. Here's the scene: the final stages of a major cup competition; one team up by a goal; the match in the balance, with the team that scores next sure to win the tie. In a congested penalty area, the ball finds its way to an attacker's feet, and the ball's launched goalwards, soaring past the goalkeeper who's straining for it like a drowning man grasping at driftwood, and the ball clatters the crossbar, spearing downward towards the goal line, raising a small puff of powdered paint as it meets the sun-chapped earth – and cries of different tones slip from the mouths in the crowd, some of celebration, some of hope, some of despair. Did the ball cross the line? Was it a goal? Meanwhile, the ball is sliced clear, and all eyes quickly turn to the arms of the referee, awaiting his signal.

Anyone who recognised the above as the 1966 World Cup final, in which England, leading 2–1 against West Germany, had a hotly-disputed goal granted in their favour, would be only half right. Geoff Hurst's controversial strike certainly fits the description provided, but a similar event occurred many miles north of Wembley thirty-one years later. It was the semi-final of the 1997 FA Cup, with Chesterfield leading Middlesbrough by two goals to one; the ball had just collided with the crossbar, and with fate into the bargain. On this occasion, however, the match officials disallowed what David Elleray would later confess to be a perfectly good goal. Middlesbrough eventually escaped with a 3–3 draw, moving effortlessly through to the final after a 3–0 victory in the replay.

I asked Andy Morris, the scorer of Chesterfield's first goal in that match, how things could've turned out if the goal had been allowed. Having retired, Morris was now working for them as as their Football in the Community Officer; I found him still in reflective mood, as if he'd considered many times the parallel paths that his life could have taken. 'I keep thinking: what if I'd kept my arms up like that England player in 1966 and caught the ball?', he said. Instead, though, Middlesbrough allowed no break in play but carried on as if there was no question that the ball had crossed the line, a professionalism which, Morris felt, may have tipped the decision against Chesterfield. 'It's hard because lower-league teams have a raw deal with decisions', he observed. 'And you just don't know what would have been. It could have changed a lot of careers for the lads. They could have been jumping all over us with the endorsements.' Had they proceeded to the final at Wembley, Chesterfield would've been the first team from the lower two divisions to have done so in the competition's history. But, as Morris noted, 'When lower-league teams meet Premier League teams, you only have one chance to beat them.'

There's a track by a French rap group, IAM, which explores perfectly the subject of luck. IAM, or 'Imperial Asiatic Men', hail from Zinedine Zidane's hometown of Marseille, their sound typically bearing the same scars and sensitivity as did the play of their fellow native son; *Nés Sous La Même Étoile* is no exception. The narrator, against the backdrop of a sorrowful cello, movingly meditates upon why his hard path of fate has been so different from that of other, more fortunate souls. 'In life, nobody's playing with the same cards', he sighs, 'too bad, I wasn't born under the same star'. Acclaimed when it was released in the late 1990s, it's a 'what if?' hymn for the ages. It's also a track with whose lyrics too many unfortunate footballers will identify. Luck is, it seems, so often what separates the have from the have–not, and players down the years appear to have acknowledged this.

In 1972, Hunter Davies asked the Tottenham Hotspur squad, 'In order of importance, which of these are necessary for a successful professional footballer: confidence, coaching, luck, perseverance, personality, physical toughness, skill?' Of the seventeen players that he asked, four put luck first of all; ten of the seventeen thought that luck was more important than coaching. Only one of them, Ray Evans, ranked luck last of all, and he was wholly contemptuous of it as a factor. 'I don't believe in luck', he told Hunter. 'All the rest of these things are facts. Luck's not a fact. Footballers are always talking about luck but it's just an excuse. I'm waiting for a break, not for luck.' A right-back, Evans replaced Joe Kinnear (who'd later go on to manage Luton and Wimbledon) for part of the 1972 season; his attitude marked him out as atypically confident, and he'd have had little time for the operatic woes of IAM. His team-mates, by contrast, almost all had superstitions of one sort or another. One of them wore the same clothes to every match, one was always third out on to the pitch, and one of them – Roger Morgan, the most extreme – said that 'I always have chewing gum to go on the pitch, but I spit it out before the game starts. As I spit it out, I try to kick it. If I hit it well, I'll have a good game. I've lots of superstitions. When they don't work, I change them.'

Roger Morgan was deeply neurotic, but then again he knew what he had to lose; a footballer's career hangs on a knife-edge whenever he steps onto the pitch, and it could fall away due to injury at any moment. To become a great player a footballer requires a stage or an event where he can manifest that greatness. Regardless of who you are, it takes no small amount of fortune to reach that stage, and football is subject to the whims of fate far more than other disciplines. From Ben Markovits, in a perceptive essay that explores the differences between UK and US sports, there's the following passage:

And this is what American sports have been designed to reward: the better athlete. America's big three (baseball, football, basketball) have evolved in order to minimise the role of luck in deciding their outcomes. Not so for English sports …. A soccer match turns on the outcome of half a dozen passages of play. Commentators talk about deserving a result, precisely because there's such a wide gap between deserts and rewards. An American would ask: if you were going to leave in doubt the question of who's better, why did you play the game? This is why American sports are made up of so many repeated moments: to ensure that every game is won or lost according to the standards of statistical relevance. A basketball game is determined by the outcome of – let's say on average – 200 shots on goal. The difference between a 50 per cent success rate and a 51 per cent success rate has every chance to make itself felt. A football match can turn on four or five: Manchester United can dominate the FA Cup final and still lose on penalties to an inferior Arsenal side. It isn't fair, but English sports, certainly in the era of the Premiership, aren't designed to be fair.

All sports are deliberately tragic, but football takes the biscuit. It's easy to criticise American sport for its endless calibration of facts, its relentless analysis of player performance as if its athletes were publicly-traded company stock – which they almost are – but one thing that American sport never needs to say is 'may the best man win', because the best man always does. Football, on the other hand, is a game whose pivotal moments occur relatively rarely, so the margin between success and failure, between making it and falling short, is thinner than a winger's ankle.

Gordon Hill thought so, and when I discussed with him the findings of my questionnaire he expressed real surprise. 'How [do people think] they get to that point where they can be a great player?', he asked. In Hill's view, there were so many obstacles to overcome before someone even reached the professional ranks that luck had to be a significant factor. And whilst some might claim that the cream always rises, it's revealing that most of those who felt that luck was unimportant weren't speaking from positions within the game. When Hill noted that 'to go forward in this game, you've got to have somebody who believes in you', he reminded me of my conversation with Andy Morris, who'd played alongside Kevin Davies during that Cup run at Chesterfield. Morris noted that, even after a string of goals in that period, Davies had attracted serious attention from only one manager, and that was Southampton's Graeme Souness. Davies eventually ended up as a mainstay of a Bolton team in the top half of the Premiership, but an alternative, less glamorous outcome was all too probable.

Whilst most great players emerge one at a time, some have had the fortune to be part of the same close-knit team, their paths to glory already mapped out with reasonable clarity.

McManaman had commented that Zidane, surrounded by fewer great players, wouldn't have been the same Zidane. Wakeling spoke of the superb Leeds United team of the late 1960s and early 1970s, in which the myriad talents (such as Paul Madeley, Eddie Gray, Allan Clarke and Peter Lorimer) and tyrants (such as Jack Charlton and Norman Hunter) complemented each other perfectly. John Giles, whom the Irish FA commended to UEFA as their best player of the past fifty years, benefited most from this state of affairs; having left Manchester United at the age of twenty-two, he met the similarly fiery Billy Bremner, and they swiftly developed into one of the most productive centre-midfield pairings in the English game. Giles and Bremner, who between them saw Leeds to two league championships in 1969 and 1974 and several other near misses in both domestic and Continental football, were a great example of the importance of partnership.

Whilst not wishing to reduce the role of managers in forming a successful team – and the sharp-witted Don Revie at Leeds ensured that the Yorkshire club's dominance was no happy accident – there's much luck entailed in just how well two players will hit it off on the pitch. Great as Franco Baresi was, you wonder how much less he'd have achieved without Billy Costacurta alongside him; and when, say, Kenny Dalglish and Ian Rush were brought together at Liverpool, there was no telling just how effective they'd be. True, there were strong indications – Dalglish's past as a Celtic legend was a decent hint – but there have been many high-profile striking couples whose marriages, though ideal at first glance, transpired to be less than perfect. Robbie Fowler and Stan Collymore, who in the mid-1990s stepped into the roles of Rush and Dalglish, were one such failure, the blame in this case falling at the feet of the scintillating but idiosyncratic Collymore.

Hill reminded me of what had happened at Old Trafford in the early 1990s, where the alchemy of champions had fallen into Sir Alex Ferguson's lap. Manchester United's youth team had miraculously yielded five future England internationals, in the forms of Paul Scholes, the brothers Gary and Phil Neville, Nicky Butt and David Beckham. There was also, in the same age group, the small matter of the Welshman Ryan Giggs. As Hill observed:

> If you look at what Alex Ferguson was handed from the youth policy... you'd say he'd won the lottery. If you tried to buy those players on the open market, it would cost you telephone numbers and telephone numbers ... most academies say they'd be happy with one player coming through. When I was running [the academy] at Chester I'd have been happy with one player, maybe two players, looking to go into the first team, and they weren't even of the calibre of United. But *six players*! (I could almost hear Hill shaking his head down the telephone line.) Six players, all of a sudden!

Similar incredulity was heard in the voice of Alan Hansen at the start of the 1995–6 season, when Manchester United lost 3–1 away to Aston Villa in their first game. Hansen, in a moment that passed swiftly into legend, professed bemusement that Manchester United had fielded such a young line-up; he commented that they couldn't win anything with kids. In a facetious sense, he was right; the Old Trafford side couldn't win just anything, they could win everything, and they did, culminating in a treble of UEFA Champions League, Premiership and FA Cup in 1999, and three consecutive Premiership titles between 1999 and 2001.

Had Hansen given a glance to recent history, he might not have embarrassed himself as he did. Only two years previously, and only a few hundred miles to the north-west, another youth academy had borne equally glorious fruit. Ajax, in their UEFA Champions League-winning side of 1995, fielded a team whose average age was twenty-two, a figure that would have plummeted yet further were it not for the presence in the side of Danny Blind and Frank Rijkaard, by then both elder statesmen in their early thirties. Louis van Gaal's side, despite (or because of) its youth, remained almost peerless in European football for two years, only narrowly failing to retain its trophy due to a loss on penalties to Juventus in the 1996 final. Following that defeat, the team was broken up by the customary asset-stripping that's seen whenever top European clubs come calling. Along the way to that final, one performance of theirs stands out: a 2–0 defeat of Real Madrid in the Santiago Bernabéu stadium, which earned them an ovation from the respectful home support.

It's no mean feat to tame the Bernabéu, which is as close to the old Coliseum as any venue in world sport. But Ajax brought that crowd to heel, with men either in or barely beyond their teens. Kluivert, Davids, Reiziger, Bogarde and Seedorf, five sons of Surinamese immigrants, sauntered about that Spanish turf as if they'd paid off its mortgage; whilst the de Boer twins, Frank and Ronald, provided a series of firm and precise passes for them and for Marc Overmars, a forward of matchless acceleration. They struck the crossbar three times in the first half alone, and saw two claims for valid goals ignored. Meanwhile, the ringmaster of all this was a tall, slightly gawky Finn, who often plodded here and there as if his boots were made of brick.

Jari Litmanen belongs in this chapter as much as anyone, as his career shows just how fickle the football gods can be. As Pete Reynolds wrote in response to my questionnaire: 'If you look at incredibly talented players with all required qualities that wouldn't make a top-50 list [of the greatest players ever], what did they lack? Say, perhaps, Jari Litmanen: heading to Barcelona after a great spell at Ajax, he should have had the world at his, uhm, feet. But, despite the odd majestic performance (if you hadn't noticed, I'm a fan), he fell from the limelight because he didn't fit new systems following managerial changes.'

The statistics speak even louder than Reynolds' words. In seven years at Ajax, Litmanen won four domestic titles and three domestic cups to go with his club's Continental success; during that period, he played 159 league games and scored 91 goals, an exceptional record for someone whose chief role was the provision of chances for others. Yet in the following eight seasons, which included a brief return to Ajax, Litmanen played only 101 league games and scored only 20 goals.

Litmanen's health had held up long enough for him to pass through football's brutal filter, that moment of truth in a player's late teens when he'll find himself either with a professional contract or on the lonely road to obscurity. But Gianluca Vialli, in *The Italian Job*, considers that the division between success and failure is more significant than I would suggest:

> I don't know if it's something that happens to all ex-footballers or if it's just me, but people seem to love to come up to me and tell me [that] they could have played professionally. They could have played internationally ... Juventus or Manchester United or Real Madrid wanted them to come on trial. But then ... it just didn't work out. And it had nothing to do with them ... Far be it for me to doubt the veracity of all these potential Maradonas but I suspect their excuses were just that: excuses. If you're good enough to play professionally, you're better than 99.9% of the population. And that generally means you don't fall through the cracks – particularly not in this day and age. The obvious conclusion is that most of these folks simply weren't good enough.

That's the obvious conclusion, but one that I thought was too convenient. The potential Maradonas whom Vialli attracts are familiar to us all; they never seem to have been courted by mediocre clubs, it's always one of the top European outfits. But then there's the example, close to Vialli's home, of Luigi Quarticelli, the boy tipped by AC Milan as the future of world, let alone Italian, football. The club's president, Silvio Berlusconi, came in for forceful criticism from Rob Hughes. Writing in May 1992 for *The International Herald Tribune*, he commented that '[Berlusconi] is so far ahead of his time that his club has bought the future of Luigi Quarticelli, who, his scouts insist, is the best 10-year-old there has ever been. Well now, aside from the noted fickleness of youth – never mind pre-puberty – and aside from the fact that if there is any such thing as a child star he should be left to grow in his own environment, is the great Berlusconi really in the business of child procurement?'

Apparently so, considered Hughes, who continued in equally blistering vein: 'Young Luigi looks smart and sweet in AC Milan colours', he wrote. 'It would be pleasing to think that innocence, an appealing trait in a player, might somehow survive the tender years. But already the boy knows his price – a reported cash sum of $17,500, a luxury Milan apartment for his folks – who are from southern Italy – and a job for papa.' Quarticelli's rise was something that riveted me and my twelve-year-old classmates, at the time deaf to the unpleasant nuances, let alone the blatant warning signs, of such an early transfer. As a result, we didn't heed Hughes' furious words of caution:

> The mind boggles at the spiral Berlusconi has thus unleashed. It recoils at the prospect of Italian agents, not all of whom will have the moral scruples Milan can afford, peddling child stars off the back streets. It happens already with 14-year-olds, and the backlash of broken minds, broken bodies and broken families can be seen from Africa to Latin America to Orta Nova, where Luigi Quarticelli was once a free child.

Given the compassionate tone of his polemic, Hughes didn't seem the kind of writer who'd be keen to see his words turn out as painfully accurate prophecy. But in this Italian prodigy's case, he was sadly proved correct. When, some years later, Quarticelli's name flitted across my mind as distant and random memories will occasionally do, I tried to find out what had become of him. All that I could ascertain was that he'd spent the years between 1997 and 2000 at three clubs – Foggia, Reggina and Crotone. And, in that time, he'd apparently played only one game.

Like Quarticelli, there are a significant number of players who fail to make the cut each year, and there are indications that their ranks are growing; football remains, after all, one of the most oversubscribed careers on the planet, and managers are less inclined than ever before to take a risk on a young but unproven talent. There's also anecdotal evidence that some of the old avenues to the top of the game are closing themselves off. Stuart Pearce, who began at non-league Wealdstone and ended up with a distinguished career for Nottingham Forest and England, described himself in his autobiography as 'a tradesman who has struck it lucky', and promised a few pages later that 'certainly if I go back into management I will look around for non-league players. I would want players of the right age and with the attitude. I would give them a chance because I was given that chance myself.'

Yet, during his ill-fated tenure as manager of Manchester City, Pearce failed to field non-league players in his side, staying in safer territory with purchases of experienced internationals such as England's Darius Vassell and the USA's DaMarcus Beasley. Pearce is certainly no coward, has as much integrity as anyone in the game, being 'the good pro' of whom Eamon Dunphy so warmly wrote. But, in a world where patience with Premiership managers is as short as an English winter, he was forced to take the easy way out.

It could be argued on the one hand that there simply wasn't the quality in the lower levels of football for Pearce to be able to make that promotion. But the travails of Javier Mascherano at West Ham at the start of the 2006–7 season, whose presence and ineffectual play seemed to damage the team, have shown that, in the wrong setting, even footballers of the richest talent can play like paupers. When that's borne in mind, it makes you wonder how many future stars were broken by rejection on the verge of fame. As Dunphy made clear, football wasn't a sport where, in such an event, they could expect much tenderness. 'The way the game treats young players is a disgrace', he wrote. 'It is one of the really shameful aspects of the game. Not only that they are not doing well as players, but that they aren't getting any preparation for the inevitable end when they are eighteen or nineteen or twenty.' Dunphy then proceeded to tell the brief tale of a boy who was released by Millwall:

The kid was sitting out on the wall by the touchline, crying. I just happened to go out and saw him. I tried to tell him that this was not the end of the road, and he could still have a decent life, that football is only a game, and so on. But it meant nothing to him at the time. In the end I got him fixed up with a catering class at the college. I think he was going to try and become a chef. I don't know whether it worked out or not. You don't. They just go, and that is the last you see of them.

A teenager shuffling off into an uncertain sunset: that was a haunting image, and one that Lee Hodges might have resembled when he left West Ham. Courted by Manchester United, Arsenal and Everton, Hodges had been an excellent prospect, a creative midfielder who represented England nine times at schoolboy international level. A local boy who lived about a mile from Upton Park, he'd trained alongside Rio Ferdinand, Eyal Berkovic, Paolo di Canio ('who angered me because he always moaned') and Joe Cole, whom as a player he found 'remarkable, the best thing I've ever seen'. All seemed set for a prestigious spell in the top flight, until the sudden descent of injury's guillotine. 'Seven knee operations in five or six years', sighed Hodges, who regarded professional football as 'the best life in the world'.

Given his love of the game, and my own, I was amazed that he was so sanguine about the cards he'd been dealt; I should have recommended that he listen to IAM. 'Lots of people can't believe I'm so calm about it', he admitted, 'but they see football as the be-all and end-all'. He clearly didn't, his worst moment in the game having been when he was coming to the end of his contract at Bristol Rovers, inevitably dogged by injury, and with a pregnant girlfriend. He recalled the difficulty of such times: 'People don't realise that you're making £400 to £500 a week, and then you're finished at thirty. The most I was ever on was £900 a week ... and from my group, Frank Lampard and Joe Cole were the only ones that really made it.'

Steve McManaman didn't buy my theory that there were countless gems lying buried deep within the reserve teams of the English game; he had faith in the country's scouting system. 'If you're good enough, you'll certainly get the opportunities', he said. 'When we were playing, we've known players, the likes of Michael Owen when he was fifteen, sixteen, Carragher, Gerrard, and we knew: he'll play for the first team one day, he'll play for the first team one day, he'll play for England. It's the same now. We could look at a player right now and we'd know like that' – he clicked his fingers – 'that he wasn't good enough. You can see.' And he couldn't have been more emphatic about the gulf in quality between different levels of the game. 'I get people saying to me all the time, "he's a good player, he could make it as a pro", but the difference between professionals and semi-pros is just, you know, *huge*. I mean, the difference between Zidane and a normal professional footballer is just... ' He paused. 'Extraordinary. You can't even imagine the likes of it. People say to me, "look at that Sunday-league player, he's a good player, him, he'd make it in the Premiership", but the difference between the Premiership and the Championship [in terms of the time you have to make decisions] is a couple of seconds, and as you go higher it's more, and more, and more.'

Dan Thomas, an academy coach for Under 12s at Millwall FC, was as unmoved as McManaman by my belief in luck. 'To be honest, when talking about the truly great, world-class players, I don't think that luck plays a very big part at all... the talent shines through so strongly that any scout or club cannot fail to notice it. I remember watching a video of Maradona when he was about ten, juggling a football and tennis ball and you could see how gifted he was – you just knew that he was going to be a star. The same with the advert for Ronaldinho which showed him as a young kid playing Futsal [a version of indoor football, played with a size-four ball] – he was head and shoulders above the rest and you could see he was special. These players have an exceptional natural God-given talent that will carry them through the system and negate the impact of luck.'

Thomas, who was working towards the acquisition of his UEFA 'A' Coaching Licence, had seen that God-given talent at first hand. He'd encountered Steven Gerrard and Michael Owen in his playing days for Cardiff and then Wales Schools, and recalled that 'they were clearly a great deal better than everyone else, and you could see that they were going to be special. There are some exceptionally talented players who slip through the net and end up in the lower leagues, but I believe that they lacked the strong psychological components of mental toughness and self-belief, and they probably didn't have the exceptional technical ability of the top players.'

The arguments of Thomas and McManaman for the most part held true; but at the back of my mind there was still the doubt thrown up by the downfall of Quarticelli. There were also the words of Craig Simmons and Stuart Smith in 'Thinking inside the box', their article for *Inside Knowledge* magazine in April 2004. In that piece, where they discussed the scouting techniques used by the Football Association in the UK to unearth and nurture elite players, they wrote that:

> The culture of professional football can be quite closed ... Tightly constructed networks are often difficult to innovate in, which may explain why innovation in the English game is perceived to occur slowly ... In some ways the closed culture gives the professional game strength. The experience of club scouts, coaches and managers is invaluable for spotting the talented boy in the local park. They see the potential where the layman would just see a child chasing a ball. Coaches and ex-players also have the tacit experience of what it takes to be a professional player. *The flip side is that the closed culture and patterning potentially lead to the slow adoption of new ideas and possibly an inability to spot talented players that do not fit previous patterns.*

What concerned me was that the young English player with an unhurried, Continental style of play might not be able to make it through the ranks. His calibrated approach to the game might be misinterpreted as casual; that's what, after all, happened to McManaman, one of the most Continental players that England has produced in recent times. Many overseas players are criticised for being unable to 'hack the Premiership' in their first season, but in reality they all need a little time for adjustment to the game's pace and its uniquely alarming tempo. Some of the English game's foremost foreign stars can report such difficult transitions. Chelsea's Didier Drogba, although he won two league championships in his first two seasons, didn't consistently show the form that convinced José Mourinho to buy him from Olympique Marseilles until his third season.

Others, such as Hugo Viana, arrive with immense reputations but drift quickly into obscurity. In 2002 Viana went to Newcastle United from Sporting Lisbon, where he was Europe's Young Player of the Year. Having been signed for £8.5 million, he left two years later for £1.5 million, having looked largely like a fish out of water. More recently at St James's Park another gifted Iberian, the attacker Alberto Luque, has suffered the same fate. I suggested to Vic Wakeling that a player in the style of Juan Román Riquelme might have had a hard time of it if he was born somewhere like, say, Bolton. 'You're probably right', said Wakeling. 'It's a very, very good example to take him, and whether he'd break through at Bolton, where Sam [Allardyce] works ever so hard, but there's nobody coming through. Middlesbrough won the FA Youth Cup last season, or the season before; they've got a couple coming through – at Everton, I'm not sure that anybody came through apart from Rooney... It is strange, and it is a worry for English football.'

Whilst scouts, coaches and managers have an eye for talent, it still doesn't mean that they'll be able to use it once they've identified it. Great players don't arise all by themselves; they each need a coach whose vision of how the game should be played is the same as their own, someone who won't force them into a system or process of development that doesn't suit them. As Simon Kuper reminded me, even the brilliant German Jürgen Klinsmann was mocked in training sessions by his team-mates, nicknamed Flipper because of his poor first touch, the ball so often bouncing off his clumsy feet. But, of course, Klinsmann evolved into a World Cup-winning forward. It was only because of a manager's faith and patience that players could truly develop their potential, and it was in meeting such a coach that the luck came into it. Vic Wakeling observed that Kevin Keegan's career owed much to Bill Shankly's support and the decision to play him up front alongside the more muscular John Toshack.

On that same reasoning, Thierry Henry is one of the luckiest players in the top flight. Arsène Wenger first employed him as a winger at Monaco, from where, after promising beginnings, he was sold to Juventus. Here, however, Henry stagnated, finding himself on the wing, and on the margins of this Italian team. It was then that Wenger, by then the manager of Arsenal, saw a way that he could best use Henry's unique gifts, and signed him again. When Henry came to Highbury, Wenger asked him to play instead as the team's primary striker, with the result that the Frenchman has become one of the most devastating forwards in world football: progressing from an average of less than one goal in five games in Monte Carlo and Turin to two goals every three games in north London. Several other players were revived or resurrected altogether by Wenger, the most grateful of whom was probably George Weah. In 1995, the Liberian became the first and only player to have been named the World, European and African Footballer of the Year; at the presentation ceremony, so great was the debt that he felt he owed to Wenger that he called him from the crowd and invited him onstage alongside him.

So you're unlucky if you don't find the coach of your dreams. It's often said that another way in which a potentially great player can be denied the stage that he deserves is through his citizenship. There are several footballers – like, indeed, George Weah – who, due to their country's mediocrity in the FIFA rankings, have not appeared or will never appear at the World Cup. As Derek Dougan memorably wrote of George Best, 'Restricted by nationality, he remained an outsider, never able to reach the centre of top international football events. It was like an actor such as John Gielgud being denied the National Theatre stage and forced to appear on the fringe with a small workshop company.'

If it's considered that a player's legacy can only be sealed by producing miracles in the World Cup, then that's a theory which, increasingly, carries too much weight. Brian Glanville, in revising his list of the world's 100 greatest footballers for *The Times*, did his best to discredit it. He wrote that 'if the blue riband of football is success in the World Cup finals, then neither Di Stefano nor Best, who never competed in them, could be considered, but their talents surely transcend such trivialities.' That must be right. Unlike many other sports, football has two tournaments of equal quality (if not prominence) during which a player's worth can be assessed: the World Cup and the Champions League. A non-appearance at the World Cup is therefore no damning indictment of a footballer.

It could even be strongly argued that the UEFA Champions League is a competition of superior pedigree. Whilst the World Cup is compelled to admit teams from each continent, and thus those nations from Africa and Asia who have significantly lower rankings than their European counterparts, market forces have dictated that the majority of the world's outstanding footballers have found their way to European clubs. The UEFA Champions League, moreover, is a stern season-long examination of the finest talent on the world stage, as opposed to the World Cup: a series of knock-out matches every four years where, to be successful, a team's fitness, luck and technique must all coincide for just one month. Best and di Stefano were indeed unlucky not to have competed at the World Cup, as, latterly, was George Weah. But the real misfortune was that of the spectators who, because they didn't have channels that broadcast European football, never had the privilege of seeing them play.

Up in Liverpool, as my coffee was slowly puffing itself lukewarm, Bolo Zenden was musing over the misfortunes that a life in football could bring a player. I'd suggested that it was a tremendous life; he'd agreed, in the main, but pointed out the drawbacks. Where I'd seen fame and wealth so young, he'd seen the loss of innocence. 'At the age of eighteen, I entered the adult world', he said; 'whereas you', he said, nodding towards me, 'you're eighteen, you finish your school, then you go to university, you have another six, seven years of fun, which you can enjoy with your mates, have a drink, have a laugh; and when you're twenty-five, twenty-six, when you've finished your studies, *that's* when reality hits you and you have to start working.'

Finishing my studies at *twenty-six* … I didn't want to resort to rigid cultural stereotypes, but the Dutch educational system as he described it did sound very relaxed; if someone had offered me four extra years of university, instead of endless months spent becoming more and more of a nonentity in the City, I'd have been laughing all the way to the college bar. But I took his point. 'Whereas', continued Zenden, almost wearily, 'if you're a youngster [like I was], you're seventeen, eighteen, you've

186

finished school, and you enter the adult world; because all of a sudden everybody knows you, you're in the papers; people look at you, at what you do and what you don't' ... He checked himself then. 'But I'm not complaining', he said, a point that he was at pains to make throughout our chat. 'I've got a fantastic job, where I've had the opportunity to kick a ball.'

Vision

He's in Japan for the 2002 World Cup, in the stadium at Shizuoka; the crowd's eyes are fixed on his right foot, each twitch of his toes scrutinised by one-hundred-thousand eyes. He is Ronaldo de Assis Moreira, or Ronaldinho, who'll soon be recognised not once but twice as the world's best footballer. For now, though, he's got at least two other things on his mind. One of these, probably, is that it's a pivotal moment in this quarter-final match between Brazil and England; although the game is tied at one apiece, it's far from a stalemate, with football's fates still to decide which way they'll ultimately cast their favour. Ronaldinho's other major concern is what he's going to do with this direct free kick that his team has been awarded near England's goal. Well, in truth, it's not that near – it's over thirty yards out, and it's some distance to the right of the goalkeeper's posts, so an attempt on goal is pretty much out of the question. Pretty much.

If Ronaldinho thought like most players, or even like David Beckham, he'd try to clip a cross into the penalty area, towards the head of one of his tall centre-backs. But maybe he's got a different idea. He approaches the ball with short, swift steps, and strikes it hard and high, the gentle loop of its flight disguising its speed. Among those initially fooled by the ball's arc is David Seaman, who's now viewing its arrival with steadily increasing dread, and who's caught in an awkward scramble back to his line as it steals beneath the crossbar and into the few square feet of net that he's left unguarded. Seaman collapses against the goal's frame in horror as Ronaldinho's moment of inspiration carries Brazil through this game and beyond, on to their fifth World Cup triumph.

But, I wondered, did Ronaldinho mean to score this impossible goal?

After the match, England's players expressed little doubt on this topic. David Seaman thought that 'he miskicked the free kick and I misjudged it'. His teammates were more effusive. David Beckham called it 'a fluke goal', Trevor Sinclair referred to it as 'a freak goal', and reserve goal-keeper David James called it 'a freak goal, a fluke'. Michael Owen, perhaps because he was interviewed last and wanted to provide journalists with some unique and fresh-sounding copy, cleverly collated all of his colleagues' responses and said: 'They scored with a freak free kick'. Ronaldinho, perhaps predictably, claimed that there was no luck involved at all.

This episode was, ultimately, a debate about vision; which is, roughly speaking, the ability to see or even to sense options on a football pitch that most of your teammates – and opponents – cannot. The England team's blanket refusal to believe that Ronaldinho's goal was intentional was largely due to the fact that, in their view, the Brazilian lacked both the skill and the imagination to consider shooting from that distance and that angle. They might yet have been right. But what their incredulous reaction shows is that there is a set of possibilities that most footballers, from the level of casual kickabouts in the park up to the World Cup finals, accept when they step onto the field of play: there are things that can be done with a football, and then there are things that simply can't. That's why, when Marco Van Basten achieved his sensational volley in the final of the 1988 European Championship against Russia, there was a split-second of silent incomprehension amongst all the spectators; in one languid swing of his right leg, this player had redefined the game.

Players who have the vision to attempt these extraordinary acts are often as amazed by their talents as anyone else. At the Euro'96 tournament, a few years after van Basten's work of art against Russia, Paul Gascoigne scored a goal against Scotland to rival the Dutchman's effort, using his left foot to lob the ball over Colin Hendry – at that time, arguably the finest centre-back in the English game – and then stroking the ball home with his right. The goal itself was marvellous, but what was almost as telling was the identical expression of the two players. When the ball floated over Hendry's head, the Scot's face was contorted in disbelief; as Hendry wheeled unsteadily round to follow its flight, Gascoigne had disappeared from view, the burly, thundering Geordie having slipped behind his back and suddenly become as ghostly as a morning mist. When Hendry next saw Gascoigne, the ball was nestled comfortably in the corner of the Scottish net, and Gascoigne, fresh from this burst of brilliance, was wearing the same astonished look as Hendry had only moments before. It was as if he was leaping up and down in a million English living rooms with everyone else, as if he had temporarily transcended himself, and was thinking: 'That Paul Gascoigne ... I have never seen anything like him'. Diego Maradona, in his autobiography *El Diego*, talks of being similarly bemused and almost humbled by his own genius. In the frank fashion that is his trademark, he discusses his miraculous dribble against England in the quarter-final of the 1986 World Cup, widely regarded as the finest individual goal ever scored:

> [It was] the goal you dream of as a kid. In the *potrero*, when we did something like that, we used to say we'd made the opponent dizzy, that we'd made them go crazy. It was ... whenever I see it again I can't believe I managed it, honestly. Not because I scored it but because it seems a goal like that just isn't possible, a goal that you could dream of but never actually score. Now it's become a legend.

Sometimes footballers possess such a great degree of vision that they have a better view of what's happening on the field than the supporter in the cheap seats who's angrily shaking his pint and Cornish pasty at the play far below. Irish midfield legend Liam Brady, the youth development coach at Arsenal, saw such a talent in the form of the Catalan wonderkid, Cesc Fàbregas:

> Even when he arrived here as a kid he was a step ahead of the others on the field – and a coach can't teach that quality. It's knowing what you're going to do with the ball even before you get it. Fàbregas is one of those rare players who can pass a ball that, up in the stands, you won't have seen.

For Liam Brady, vision was a gift that could not be taught. It's in your nature, and there's no amount of nurture that will coax it out of a mediocre footballer. Certainly there are many who would agree with him. Kaká, the gliding, graceful midfielder of AC Milan and Brazil, and a devout evangelical Protestant, quickly became famous for pointing thankfully to the heavens after each goal. Maradona frequently referred to being inspired by God (or, as he referred to him, 'The Beard'). But is vision truly something that can't be coached? If a player can stretch his legs to loosen up his hamstrings, isn't there some way that he can work his mental muscles so that he's got more flair, more imagination?

The knee-jerk response to this last question is *no*, because it's generally held that creativity and spontaneity are uniquely human traits. The days of artificial intelligence, despite the best film-making efforts of Steven Spielberg, are still thought to be fairly far away. As a result, the thought of using a computer to give footballers the gift of vision probably strikes us as impossible. But, as a canny Ukrainian once showed, such thinking is a touch complacent.

Valery Lobanovsky, a former colonel in the Russian army, didn't set out to create a batallion of robots who would run the entire planet: instead, he confined his ambitions to the world of football. Back in the 1970s, he ordered a computer, an action sufficient to alert the KGB (and which presumably had the young Vladimir Putin sniffing through his garbage). As the coach of Dynamo Kiev, he used this device to collect comprehensive data on all of his players, from their fitness levels to the amount of times they ran with and without the ball during matches. He'd then use this information for team selection and design of training programmes, working in conjunction with Professor Anatoly Zelentsov, whom he had met in Dneprepetrowsk in the late 1960s.

Simon Kuper, in *Football Against the Enemy*, described the occasion when he had visited Zelentsov and sat through a series of such computer tests, which were designed to test and sharpen the instincts of Dynamo Kiev's players. These tests were used when Dynamo were considering signing a player, and were also used to make regular assessments of the existing members of the squad. Kuper wrote with particular awe of a test that essentially measured a player's level of vision, confessing that 'the last test I found impossible. A dot would trace a complicated trajectory through a maze, and then I had to retrace the path, using a joystick. But I could never remember the route, and the maze was so narrow and mazy, and moreover constantly in motion, that I was always bumping into walls ... it made me realise how extraordinary professional footballers are. Not after years of practice could I have negotiated that maze.'

Lobanovsky's philosophy was that of the 'universal footballer', and he considered that 'modern football is about nothing but using players' individual features for collective reasons ... There is no such thing as a striker, a midfielder, a defender. There are only footballers and they should be able to do everything on the pitch.' This mode of thinking – that each man on a team represents a part of a seamless whole, and can exchange positions with his colleagues at will – is not too far removed from the Dutch concept of Total Football, although it can easily be argued that Lobanovsky's approach was far more forensic than that of Johann Cruyff. It was also vaguely militaristic, appropriately Soviet, Lobanovsky commenting at one time that 'the tactics are not chosen to suit the best players ... they must fit our play. Everybody must fulfil the coach's demands first, and only then perform his individual mastery.' This requirement of subverting oneself to the greater good wasn't always a hit with his players, many of whom found him difficult on a personal level, but the results – a total of fifteen domestic and European titles – bore out the wisdom behind his methods. What these methods also did was show that, to some extent, vision is a quality that can be manufactured. If we briefly strip away all the romantic notions that surround this element, then we see that vision is really nothing more than a heightened awareness of what's happening around you on the pitch.

If a team is sufficiently well-drilled then its members can develop an almost intuitive familiarity. Witness the group telepathy enjoyed by the great and mostly youthful Ajax side of 1994–5, who won that season's European Champions Cup; a team where Davids, Seedorf, Kluivert and Litmanen drifted hypnotically between midfield and attack. Barry Hulshoff, of the great and slightly less youthful Ajax side of the 1970s, has cautioned against getting carried away with mystical perceptions of the way that the Dutch played their football. Speaking to David Winner for his fine work *Brilliant Orange*, he remarked that, 'You know how it goes. People couldn't see that sometimes we just did things automatically. This way of playing, we grew into it. We didn't realise the ball was going that fast, that we were changing positions so much. We knew exactly what to do because we'd known and played with each other for five years.' I would later mention Hulshoff's point to Hugh McIlvanney, who expanded upon it thus:

There's this other dimension that you never lose concentration, you never lose the sense of involvement ... and so when I'm sixty yards from the ball, I'm more likely to go to the right place because I'm thinking of my reaction to what is happening, instead of switching off as so many players do. Good players, even goalkeepers, are always involved.

But what of those footballers who are able, without much or any practice, to see and explore these patterns on the pitch? They are the true visionaries, and they are scattered throughout the game's history in what is, at first, a seemingly infinite array of moods, shapes and sizes: from the tall and brooding Juan Román Riquelme of Argentina to England's Paul Scholes, short, shy and retiring, who as a child might have been scared of his own shadow. However, on closer analysis, these players share a handful of distinctive features.

One of these is often, surprisingly, a lack of pace. Teddy Sheringham, even in his prime, was so slow that he'd struggle to beat a milk float in a short sprint; Jan Molby, a star of Liverpool's late 1980s juggernaut, was little swifter. It's difficult to reconcile this fact with the lasting influence that both of them have had in the domestic game, Molby being praised by Kenny Dalglish as one of the finest midfielders of his generation, and Sheringham winning the Treble with Manchester United in 1999. At first sight, a game as notoriously fast as the English one has no place for footballing sloths such as these. But, such is their innate feel for the flow of play, that speed is an irrelevance. Real Madrid's Fernando Redondo, who destroyed Manchester United in the 1999–2000 UEFA Champions League quarter-final, was so good at anticipating where the ball would end up that he rarely needed to make a sliding tackle, let alone break sweat. On that occasion he famously moved Sir Alex Ferguson to suspect that he wore magnets in his boots. An even greater accolade was that he was praised by Juventus, AC Milan and Real Madrid coach, and tactical perfectionist, Fabio Capello, as being 'tactically perfect'.

What's more, players who have vision (or PVs, for ease of reference) always seem to be standing in at least two yards of space. A classic case in point is Dennis Bergkamp, who achieved this despite playing much of his career at Arsenal's Highbury stadium, which was comfortably one of the smallest pitches anywhere in professional football. Bergkamp always had room. It didn't seem to matter if his man-marker had been ordered to cling to him like a film of sweat on a humid day. It didn't seem to matter if it was the dying moments of an international match, the score was tied, and half the stadium was screaming, panto fashion, 'LOOK OUT, HE'S BEHIND YOU'. On that last point, we could consult Roberto Ayala, the Argentina defender who is probably still receiving counselling for the time that Bergkamp crept up on him in the 1998 World Cup to score one of the greatest individual goals ever seen. Despite his dearth of speed, Bergkamp wandered beyond two defenders, pulled down a sixty-yard through ball with a touch as soft as cotton wool, bounced the ball under the lunging Ayala with the sole of his right boot and then clipped a half-volley into the far top corner of the net. This almost spectral ability of being able to slip away from close defensive attention and then reappear in the guts of the penalty area is the hallmark of the PV.

However, this skill of drifting in and out of games is a double-edged sword, since it means that PVs tend to be regarded with a certain amount of suspicion. Because PVs are essentially free spirits in a game which relies especially on a strong team ethic, there's often a question as to where they 'fit in' within a team. Some managers have been so paranoid about the PV's possibly adverse effect on a team that they have relegated them to the bench or dropped the poor bohemian souls altogether. (This is possibly the main reason why Glenn Hoddle, once idolised by Bergkamp himself, played a mere forty-four times for England.) PVs are frequently caricatured, perhaps unfairly, as prima donnas, and there is never any shortage of criticism when one of them falls to earth under a defender's challenge, the assumption being that they must have dived. The honourable exception to this rule is Wayne Rooney, who trained as a boxer in his early teens – not that, with his build, he needed to – and whom, short of exploring military options, it would be very tough for anyone to stop in his tracks.

The PV, then, is something of an outsider. This is perhaps reflected in the places that he hangs out on the pitch, that mark him out as a very different creature to his colleagues and opponents. Centre-backs, tied down by tactics and a keen sense of obligation, patrol their areas like armed farmers looking for trespassers. Dogged defensive midfielders, such as Claude Makalélé, are similarly moored to their posts, as, to a lesser extent, are wingers such as Ryan Giggs, one of the most selfless attackers to have played the game. But the PV is generally free from such restrictions, and is generally found on the fringes of the action until he chooses a decisive moment. If he's right-footed, he'll start out on the left wing and wander infield, and if he's left-footed, then vice-versa: a technique of torment favoured by Robert Pirès, Thierry Henry and, latterly, Arjen Robben.

Arguably the finest PV of the modern era – and this assessment includes Diego Maradona – is Zinedine Zidane, who both on and off the field perfectly fits this stereotype: closely involved in the play but at the same time magnificently aloof, elusive yet everywhere. Steve McManaman, in his autobiography *El Macca – Four Years with Real Madrid*, wrote in almost awed tones of both Zidane's gifts and his ambiguous, mysterious presence:

I like the fact that he's the best player on the planet, and yet so modest. He's so quiet. On the bus, he sits up at the front by himself, out of the way ... [After games] he'll look as if he wants to join in, but doesn't mix … In a way he's unknowable as a person … He's so elegant, yet he has a hard side …. I remember reading some French rock star saying nobody can work out if Zidane is an angel or a demon because he smiles like Mother Teresa and grimaces like a serial killer.

Given the difficulty that friends and footballing foes alike have had in trying to fathom Zidane, it's appropriate that the location on the pitch where he does his best work is referred to as 'the hole', an enigmatic term, which might be better described as 'the Bermuda Triangle of football': that gap of about twenty square feet about twenty-five yards from goal, which is just too far for defenders to venture and just too far for midfielders to track back. As such, it's no-man's-land, and it's in this unclaimed space that PVs like Zidane thrive, spinning free from challenges and flicking or chipping passes in behind the opposing rearguard.

The understanding of space is therefore the essence of what it means to have vision. This has been eloquently expressed by the Dutch artist Jeroen Henneman, speaking to David Winner of the dramatic development of his country's football:

> Football was always unconsciously about space. The good players were always the ones who instinctively found positions to receive the ball in space. But the big change in Dutch football happened when these ideas became words, when Cruyff and Michels started talking about space. No one ever looked at it in that way before …. Suddenly Cruyff was saying, 'If there is an attack and this person runs to the side of the field, he will attract a defender who goes with him, so there is room for a midfielder to run in and score'. And because they talked about it, it opened a whole vista of seeing football totally differently.

Most PVs tend to wear the number-ten shirt, a position where they have the great responsibility of setting the rhythm of their team's football, of making its play. The nature of a number-ten's game, which is to work within and between the cracks of well-briefed defences, is one which often runs contrary to the ethos of modern football, as lamented by Richard Williams in his *The Perfect 10: Football's Dreamers, Schemers, Playmakers and Playboys*. He considered that 'with the increased pace of the game and the reduced amount of space available for self-expression has come a premium on the sort of instant skill and appreciation of angles and distances that is available only to the greatest players in any generation'. In this view, therefore, the playmaker risks being squeezed out of the game. The improved fitness of contemporary footballers means that most managers can rarely afford to field one, let alone two, players who would like to take more time on the ball. This, in theory, makes defending easier, as the playmaker can be isolated ever more swiftly than before; yet the playmaker continues to prosper, as he relies increasingly on his speed of thought. Majid Abdullah, probably the finest footballer to have emerged from the Middle East, agreed with this sentiment when I spoke with him, equally concerned that the speed of modern football meant that truly innovative footballers were a dying breed. 'These days, coaches don't let players have time to think', he said, almost wistfully. 'They just make them run here, here and there, like robots.'

The modern number-ten is therefore unlikely to take more than two or three touches in possession of the ball. However, this could yet lead to a simplicity of approach that is in many ways the epitome of precise yet stylish football that was the hallmark of the Brazil World Cup side of 1970, and of the Real Madrid legends of the 1950s.

Why then, comes the familiar and inevitable refrain, are there so few English players blessed with the quality of vision? The answer is found in the type of midfielder that is revered in the British game, exemplified in the 1980s and 1990s by Bryan Robson and Roy Keane, and more recently Steven Gerrard and Frank Lampard. This quartet are among the finest box-to-box midfielders that the United Kingdom and the Republic of Ireland have ever seen, and are therefore held up as the benchmark for those who play in their position. They became known and loved for their ability to pass, run, tackle and score – for their ability to do it all; and this is precisely the problem. Just because a midfielder can do it all, it does not mean that he should; otherwise, the temptation emerges to become an all-action master of all trades. Routinely expected to achieve exceptional ratings in the categories of shots attempted, defensive clearances made and distance covered, the English midfielder ends up either falling far short of success or – even worse – excelling, so that the game is always played at a high and exhausting tempo. As a result, there is less room for the visionary players to roam.

English football fans are particularly proud of the work ethic of their players. It's vital that they go about the game with pride and passion, that they wear their hearts on their sleeves, that they run their socks off. A great value has been placed upon conspicuous toil, and too often it has been the case that footballers work hard instead of working smart. In October 2001, England met Greece at Old Trafford in a World Cup qualifying match, in the knowledge that a draw would take them through to the finals to be jointly hosted by Japan and South Korea. That day, most of the home team had fallen prey to that odd mix of smugness and supreme self-doubt that affects many English national sides in the face of destiny, and it took a performance of superhuman endeavour from David Beckham to save them. In the course of the match, he ran seven miles, created a goal for Teddy Sheringham, and scored a last-minute equaliser for a 2–2 draw, a majestic free kick from thirty yards which thundered into the top left-hand corner. But his efforts set a misguided standard for English midfielders in the years to come, one which neither he nor his teammates would be able to match again.

This culture of can-do-everything has harmed Steven Gerrard more than most when playing for England. Whilst he has had wonderful success for Liverpool, playing the starring role in FA Cup and UEFA Champions League triumphs, the more patient approach required at major tournaments has often proved his undoing. A statistic from the quarter-final of the 2004 European Championship against Portugal is particularly revealing: whilst Maniche, Gerrard's opposite man, played 120 minutes and completed 79.2% of his passes, Gerrard played 80 minutes and completed 38.9% of his passes – a distribution rate that was by some distance the worst of any player on the pitch, and which did a disservice to arguably the finest English central midfielder of his generation. To watch this game was to see Gerrard, at one point, hitting a forty-yard pass to centre-forward Darius Vassell, who, being well short of six feet in height, was summarily engulfed by the centre-backs Andrade and Carvalho. To watch this game was also to see a footballer who has not, despite all that he has done for club and country, truly been allowed to enjoy himself in possession of the ball – a luxury which the thud and thunder of the Premier League does not permit, but which is essential in the later stages of the World Cup, when fatigue and tight marking turn the defensive screws ever tighter.

The suspicion that many managers have of PVs is extremely keen in England, where there seems to be a particular desire to see that players are working hard, if not always working smart. This perhaps explains the strangely truncated international career of Steve McManaman, who despite winning two league championships and two UEFA Champions League titles at Real Madrid won only 37 caps for England. Kevin Keegan explained McManaman's problem thus:

> He's very relaxed but you have to know him to understand him. His attitude is, 'I am what I am. This is me'. He is not someone who makes you think he is trying hard to impress you. He'd not come on for the last 10 minutes and make sure everyone took notice of what they'd been missing... That relaxed confidence means he can coolly control a game with his passing and running, but when the game is going against us, it is not a good manner to have. It can look like it doesn't mean enough to him.

The symbolic case of McManaman, the most successful English export in recent years, being exiled in Spain and largely absent from the England training camp, is a damning one for those who want to have their cake and eat it; for those who wish England to win the World Cup, but who would omit players such as McManaman who can direct phases of the team's play. Perversely, it may even be that Wayne Rooney's rage and Paul Gascoigne's passion have been somehow comforting for fans of the

Three Lions; that, since they had the atypically English attribute of time on the ball, it was reassuring to know that they so conspicuously cared about their football, wearing their hearts on their sleeves like any true Englishman would. However, if England wish to make their mark on the world stage soon, they might be well advised to take a more deliberate stance, and heed some of the words of the former Ajax and Holland star Arnold Muhren, who believed that football was 'a thinking game. It's not running around everywhere and just working hard, though of course you have to work hard too ... That's how to play football: with your brains, not with your feet. Before I had the ball I knew exactly what I would do with it. I always knew two or three moves ahead.' He considered, more than a touch unfairly, that 'English players don't think until they have the ball at their feet'.

Hugh McIlvanney was thoroughly unimpressed by this suggestion. 'I remember Muhren', he said, like a weary schoolmaster who's just heard that one of his old pupils has been arrested for fraud. 'Good player, but I think he's a bit cheeky there, with all that about English players not thinking until they get the ball. Muhren shouldn't be so impertinent. I mean, look at Johnny Haynes [of Fulham].' And, indeed, Sir Stanley Matthews, who in 1957 was elected as the first European Footballer of the Year. But the persistent argument that arises from Muhren's uncharitable comment is that English midfielders are not allowed to be sufficiently detached from the fray that they can become playmakers.

You might, so far, be gaining the sense that PVs have a particular attitude: an air of superiority over their fellow footballers, and occasionally a flash of contempt. This superiority isn't always manifested in an arrogant fashion: for example, Steven Gerrard's upright stance, head raised as he surges forward, is a long way down the confidence gradient from Eric Cantona's upturned collar. Yet it's a common theme that binds all PVs, evidence of the self-belief needed to do daring and spontaneous things in front of tens of thousands of paying spectators each week. Amongst Wayne Rooney's many talents, one of the most striking is his composure; in his first major international, against Turkey, he could be seen calling for the ball to feet, pointing to his toes as if it were a casual training match and not a life-or-footballing-death World Cup qualifier. The autumn after France won the World Cup in 1998, Zinedine Zidane came to Wembley and jogged gently about the pitch for ninety minutes, so leisurely in his manner that he could have been wearing a tuxedo and silk scarf. The England back four, who in retrospect should probably have been briefed to kick chunks out of the Frenchman, were transfixed as their team fell to a 2–0 thrashing.

However, a nomination for the most relaxed performance of recent times must go to Xabi Alonso, Jan Molby's spiritual heir at Liverpool, in a UEFA Champions League quarter-final against Juventus. Liverpool, defending a 2–1 lead from the first leg at Anfield, went to the Stadio Delle Alpi with Alonso at the helm of their midfield, which would ordinarily have been ideal, only that the Basque had recently returned from a long break after injury. No matter. Alonso, firing long or short passes to either wing, saw Liverpool safely through the tie as they kept possession superbly on their way to a 0–0 draw, so in command of the tempo of the match that at one point it seemed that Alonso was sitting in an armchair in the centre-circle and dictating play from there.

Given the laconic manner of players like Alonso, the calm calculation that they bring to games, it's tempting to ask whether vision is related to academic intelligence. There have certainly been players who were no slouches in the classroom. It rarely escapes mention that Albert Camus, a Nobel Laureate for Literature, was a keen goalkeeper. Socrates, of the dazzling Brazil side of the 1982 World Cup, is a qualified doctor, and even sported an intellectual-looking beard that would have suited his namesake. Following that theme, Zvonimir Boban, a subtle and stellar attacking talent for AC Milan and Croatia in the mid-1990s, has a degree in philosophy, and Frank Lampard Jr has joked that he must be the only footballer with an A* in Latin GCSE.

But counter-examples of this trend are not too difficult to find. Francesco Totti, Roma's sublime *fantasista* (an Italian word for PV), is famed in Italy for his lack of native wit, although – to his eternal credit – he recently published a book of jokes lampooning his supposed dumb-ness. David Beckham, who in terms of vision went one better than Pelé when he scored from the halfway line against Wimbledon for Manchester United, has often spoken of his disinterest in school.

Debates on the connection between vision and academic intelligence have the potential to turn swiftly nasty, partly out of a desire to be able to ridicule athletes who are widely regarded as overpaid. But the debate is just that – academic. Short of the lifestyle demands caused by the multicultural dressing rooms of most major European football teams, it's not necessary for footballers to speak a handful of languages, as did luminaries such as Ruud Gullit and Jürgen Klinsmann. If there's going to be any useful discussion of intelligence, then it has to be framed in terms of footballing intelligence – that is to say, players who were so smart on the field of play that they were true innovators, such as Johann Cruyff. Indeed, Cruyff was such a pioneer that he's the only player to have had a skill, his turn, directly named after him. Such moves, however, are mere expressions of vanity if not used in the proper area of the pitch, and the truly intelligent players will always know when to be pragmatic and where to be flamboyant. Ultimately, the greatest examples of vision are those – be they passes, dribbles or shots – that are executed in the blink of an eye, since it's generally these spontaneous acts of brilliance that will break open the tightest of matches.

By this token, then, Zidane's quarter-final performance for France against Brazil at the 2006 World Cup in Germany must rank as one of the greatest sustained exhibitions of vision in recent times. There were several crucial facts surrounding this encounter. Brazil were the clear favourites. Ronaldo, Brazil's ailing and ageing striker, had recently become the competition's all time leading scorer, and looked ready to escape sustained criticism about his alleged complacency and dramatic weight gain; between himself and Ronaldinho, they had been awarded the title of World Player of the Year five times. Alongside them in their three-man front line stood Kaká, and in the wings waited Robinho, formerly of Pelé's Santos and now of Real Madrid, and considered to be the most gifted of them all. Zidane, although he himself had been voted the world's best player on three occasions, had retired from club football after two indifferent seasons in Madrid. Although he had produced a magical goal against Spain in the previous round, a mesmeric, drifting dribble inside Carlos Puyol and then a drive that ripped like a furious harpoon into the bottom corner, it was generally felt that this match would be his swansong as he creaked towards the exit of professional football. Worse still, in over fifty appearances alongside Arsenal phenomenon Thierry Henry, he had failed to create a single goal for him.

The connection between football and art has often, and sometimes tortuously, been made; but it is fair to say that, on that evening in Frankfurt's Commerzbank Arena, Zidane did not treat this match as a farewell script, but rather as a blank canvas on which he'd render one of his most compelling masterpieces. As a visionary would do, he saw the need to set the tone with his first touches of the match, precisely as he had done in Real Madrid's humiliation of Manchester United at the Bernabéu in the 2001–2 UEFA Champions League. Then, he had isolated and taunted David Beckham, cupping the ball in his instep, then tucking it under his heel as Beckham, an angry arm's length away, flailed both legs helplessly at him. On this occasion, as soon as the whistle for kick-off had blown, Zidane headed infield, towards Gilberto Silva and Juninho; then, with not so much a drop as a tilt of the shoulders, he seemed to evaporate beyond them, leaving them as resolute and useless as the Maginot Line.

A few minutes later, he confronted the veteran Cafu near the touchline, the once-marauding right-back who'd been dubbed *Il Pendolino* (The Commuter) for his breathless forays down the flank for AC Milan in Serie A. This time, however, the commuter was stranded in the traffic of his own confusion as Zidane rolled the ball under his right foot and then flicked it past Cafu with his left, a move so bewildering that as Malouda made his way down the left touchline with the ball Cafu was still watching Zidane's toes, perhaps fearing how much more twinkle they'd produce over the course of the ninety minutes. Towards the end of the half, he flummoxed Ronaldo by looping the ball over his head, and then heading a simple square pass to a teammate.

Although none of these three actions led to a goal, they led to something almost as important: the French team's belief that they, and not Brazil, were the favourites for this game. It seemed that Zidane had systematically set about exposing each of the icons of the Brazil team, and there was something almost inevitable about his finely-flighted fifty-seventh-minute free kick that created the game's only goal for Thierry Henry. At the final whistle, there was a great moment when Robinho ran over to embrace his former club colleague Zidane, as if to tell him that his torch would pass one day soon, but not yet. But – as Zidane would be the first to note – it shouldn't be thought that vision is all about spotting the most complex option; often, it's seeing and doing the simplest of things at a time when everyone else is caught in the thrall of adrenaline. Charles Green was the first player to show me this.

Charles was the defensive midfielder for our prep school first eleven, a blond bullet of a South African who was the anchor of this most cosmopolitan of teams: in the snow-white heart of Ascot, our coach had somehow assembled a side that featured only five indigenous Englishmen, the rest of us with roots in Greece, Sweden, Australia, Zambia and Uganda. Nick Dawson, presiding over this team that was almost as diverse as Arsène Wenger's Arsenal, blew his whistle for a corner in a practice match against the school's second eleven; the ball looped to Charles Green on the edge of his own penalty area, who then looked up to consider a counter-attack. As Green strode forward, he saw a fleet of green shirts, mine included, scuttling towards the opposition goal as swiftly as our twelve-year-old legs would carry us. We attackers were pursued by their four defenders, clad in red, so the sight that must have greeted Green at that moment was a patchwork of torsos disappearing upfield into the autumn sun, all expecting a decisive pass to be slipped into their paths. In fact, Green was so fast that he could arguably have pushed the ball thirty yards ahead of him and outpaced most of us to it: he was perhaps the most rapid sprinter at the school, who when he ran the hundred metres would hold his breath the entire distance, the tendons on his neck standing out like the ribs of a starving man.

But, having reached the halfway line, Green saw that there was no option directly ahead of him, save for lobbing it into a scrambling tangle of our forwards and their back four. So he played a simple ten-yard ball with his instep to Harry Boyle, who was our other central midfielder and, as an Englishman in our team, something of an endangered species. Dawson blew his whistle immediately, a sharp blast that brought us to an anxious standstill. When we turned back to face him, though, he was grinning as widely as any of us could remember. He pointed at Green, and then the ball, and said: 'See that? That's the best pass you'll see anywhere this season'.

For years, this was the short pass that was moored most firmly in my memory, until I witnessed one that Nick Dawson would have readily applauded. It came from Italy's Andrea Pirlo, in the 2006 World Cup semi-final against Germany in Dortmund. It was the one-hundred-and-nineteenth minute of a match that, though goalless, was marked by no little intrigue, and was a scene that recalled perfectly the call to arms of Rudyard Kipling's *If*, to keep one's head when all around were losing theirs. The ball, having been swung from the right-hand corner flag by del Piero deep into the German penalty area, was sliced anxiously to Andrea Pirlo, where it instantly fell under his influence. Pirlo was twenty yards from goal, and the goalkeeper Lehmann was unsighted by a series of toiling, tiring bodies; the temptation must have been, as he had done successfully against Ghana in an earlier round, to release a fizzing drive from the top of the box. But he saw beyond the obvious. Instead, he sidestepped one defender, sidestepped another; and then, remarkably – his head facing away from goal, his eyes fixed firmly on the right-hand touchline – he played one of the most beautiful ten-yard passes of modern times, as light in weight as that by Charles Green fifteen years before: a simple, soft side-foot into the stride of the advancing Grosso, whose left foot applied such spin to the ball that, had the net not stopped it, it could have curled full circle. Italy, now a goal ahead, had taken a lead that they were not to relinquish, in fact, a lead that they were to double thanks to del Piero's late, late flamboyant finish.

These two minutes of genius that eventually led to Italy's World Cup 2006 triumph were, if anything, indicative of the lot of the PV: to spend much of their careers unfairly maligned, and then to emerge triumphantly into the spotlight, a little like that frustrated actor who finally gets the call from the Hollywood studio. Pirlo, the creator of that wonderful Grosso goal, had endured a nomad's career, wandering from Brescia to Reggina and Internazionale before finally being understood, and therefore settling, at AC Milan. Del Piero, although vastly more accomplished, had still been regarded as a *dilettante*, a performer who became strangely passive in the biggest games of all. And perhaps that's the way that it'll always be; the majority of football fans, players and coaches may forever be a little wary of those footballers who, under such pressure as were del Piero and Pirlo, will yet attempt – and execute – such audacious acts of brilliance.

Pirlo's particular gift, to be decisive when the game had come to its crux, was what two respondents to my questionnaire saw as a quality separate from vision. Alex Payne referred to it as 'timing... the ability to capture the moment, and propel a team forward single-handedly'. Timur Asar also raised the subject of timing, defining its essence as 'being in the right place at the right time, be it for the last-second tackle, save in the top corner or to head a goal, the reading of the game. In my opinion different to vision (picking out a pass).'

Asar's and Payne's views on this matter were echoed somewhat by Gianluca Vialli and Gabriele Marcotti in *The Italian Job*, a book that has compared and contrasted England's and Italy's football cultures. Vialli and Marcotti wrote that 'what makes [the great players] special is ... the instinct to do something most of us would never even contemplate. And to do it at that particular time, in that particular context. That's genius.'

For me, though, this was still vision. Vision wasn't only seeing a pass, it was seeing the correct pass at the correct time. I wanted to know more about what a great player would see in his mind at a time like this, so I asked Andy Barton whether it was true, that footballers were on the whole less intelligent than average. 'Oh, God, no', he answered. 'With elite sportspeople, across the board, I have never met one who hasn't got a fantastic imagination, whatever sport it is. That's one reason they're great to work with ... I was working with one guy recently who was [thinking] back to a goal he'd scored and he had the biggest smile you've ever seen in your life. I mean, he was *there*.'

That's the kind of focus that you needed to process several options per second; it was so impressive a capacity that it demanded respect. If footballing brains were computers, then that of the average amateur footballer was an abacus, and that of Wayne Rooney was a Pentium chip. Players like him, Barton explained, are 'playing really positive movies in their heads, [which are] really vivid and very real, and they're hearing really loud sounds; it's like they're in the most fantastic cinema... That's what the difference is.'

Vision's a virtue that is universal among great sportsmen, and is often displayed in a champion's signature move. For example, you might have a Pete Sampras backhand pass in the middle of a close tie-break, or a Tiger Woods pitching-wedge for an eagle at the 16th; back in football, there was always Roberto Baggio and his endless gallery of swirling strikes from far beyond the edge of the box. The only problem with pulling off such manoeuvres is that, if you're not yet an established name in the sport, people will think that you've fluked it. To be acknowledged as a true visionary, a miracle maker, you need a track record of terrific deeds. This is why, in some quarters, the jury was out for some time on Wayne Rooney, even after his magnificent last-minute drive to defeat Arsenal in 2002; he was only seventeen, and English football had seen many a false dawn before. This is also one of the main reasons why Ronaldinho's World Cup free kick against England was so frowned upon in 2002: he was an upstart, a buck-toothed Brazilian who hadn't paid his dues. Was this free kick an act of true genius, or was Ronaldinho merely another false prophet?

The answer to this lies in our final illustration of the art of vision, brought to us by a familiar face. Having paid his dues, he's in west London in 2004, on a reasonably cold night, far from the soft press of the Continental breeze that greets him most weeks as he goes about his work. It's the quarter-final of Europe's most prestigious tournament, the UEFA Champions League, and it's a critical point in the match; he's on the edge of the opposition's area, looking to make a swift pass to a silver-shirted colleague, but he's faced by an endless barrier of blue uniforms. As that wave approaches he's stuck in the hole, the Bermuda

Triangle, marooned; and then, in his words, 'It seems like someone pressed pause and for three seconds all the players on the pitch have stopped and I am the only one that moves.' What he sees, between the edge of that onrushing tide and the goalkeeper's right-hand post, is a space no wider than the heart of a car tyre, and so from fully twenty yards he jabs his toe through the line of the ball with tremendous force. He scores, and the net ripples, almost in applause. Over the next week, Ronaldinho's strike against Chelsea is described in delirious terms by the Spanish press, and this time there's no doubt expressed about his goal-scoring intentions, despite the other-worldly level of technique that was needed to bring about this moment. He's the World Player of the Year now, and there's no more talk of fluke goals, or freak goals, or any of the rest of it: there's talk only of invention, and of vision.

Afterword

All of the greatest footballers must have these eleven elements, but it's still not that simple. The path to greatness, down which most players wander only a couple of paces, is one with two stages: emergence and escape.

We all know, and we've all felt, the first: when a young footballer emerges upon the scene, forcing the world to double-take in wonder at a perfect performance of his, or even just a perfect goal. We'll replay those highlights endlessly in our dreams or on our DVDs, hoping that in time he'll show us more of the same moments. But in reaching this stage, the footballer falls into the trap of comparison, which can hold him captive for many years. Every football fan's guilty of keeping him there. Whenever our eyes hungrily seize upon a new talent, we're quick to say who he reminds us of. We have to find a great player who came before him as a benchmark. It's not enough for, say, Cesc Fàbregas to have madness, graft, guts, and all the rest of it; he has to look like someone we've seen before.

So the statisticians will pull out the figures to match Fàbregas up against the 'pass-masters' of the past, whilst the supporters who haven't got the time or the will to crunch these numbers, who rely more on how watching a player makes them feel, will look at the Spaniard and think of the last midfielder who gave them this much joy. Therefore Fàbregas can only be great once he escapes from comparison with any other player who played in his position, so that he's simply Cesc Fàbregas instead of the next Pep Guardiola; similarly, Wayne Rooney will be truly great once he's fled the shadow of Paul Gascoigne, whilst Robinho seems for now to have been swallowed by that of Pelé. Steven Gerrard is already there, having escaped Bryan Robson; Michael Owen lingers on a par with Lineker; Thierry Henry, in the space of just six years at Arsenal, soared beyond Ian Wright.

Which goes to show that though all great players have my eleven elements in their DNA, they're all infinitely different. The blueprint of Roberto Baggio is nothing like the blueprint of Best, or Beckenbauer: these footballers define the way that the game is to be played, and, in doing so, they each make their own glorious journey into history.

Select Bibliography

Ball, Phil, *White Storm: 100 Years of Real Madrid*, Edinburgh, Mainstream, 2002

Ballague, Guillem, *A Season on the Brink: Rafael Benitez, Liverpool and the Path to European Glory*, London, Weidenfeld & Nicolson, 2005

Barend, Frits and van Dorp, Henk, *Ajax Barcelona Cruyff*, London, Bloomsbury, 1998

Barnes, Simon, *The Meaning of Sport*, London, Short Books, 2006

Bellos, Alex, *Futebol: The Brazilian Way of Life*, London, Bloomsbury, 2002

Burn, Gordon, *Best and Edwards: Football, Fame and Oblivion*, London, Faber & Faber, 2006

Burns, Jimmy, *Hand of God: The Life of Diego Maradona*, London, Bloomsbury, 1997

Castro, Ruy, *Garrincha: The Triumph and Tragedy of Brazil's Forgotten Footballing Hero*, London, Yellow Jersey, 2004

Conn, David, *The Beautiful Game? Searching for the Soul of Football*, London, Yellow Jersey, 2004

Davies, Hunter, *The Glory Game: Year in the Life of Tottenham Hotspur*, London, Sphere, 1973

Dunphy, Eamon, *Only a Game? Diary of a Professional Footballer*, London, Pengiun, 1987

Edworthy, Sarah, and McManaman, Steven, *El Macca: Four Years with Real Madrid*, London, Simon & Schuster, 2004

Fowler, Robbie, *Fowler: My Autobiography*, London, Macmillan, 2005

Gallacher, Ken, *Slim Jim Baxter: The Definitive Biography*, London, Virgin, 2002

Gascoigne, Paul, *Gazza: My Story*, London, Headline, 2004

Gerrard, Steven, *Gerrard: My Autobiography*, London, Bantam, 2006

Greaves, Jimmy, *The Heart of the Game*, London, Little Brown, 2005

Hunter, Norman, *Biting Talk: My Autobiography*, London, Hodder & Stoughton, 2004

Hyde, Lewis, *Trickster Makes this World : Mischief, Myth, And Art*, New York, 1997

Jenkins, Garry, *The Beautiful Team: In Search of Pele and the 1970 Brazilians*, London, Simon & Schuster, 1998

Keane, Roy, *Keane: The Autobiography*, London, Michael Joseph, 2002

Kuper, Simon, *Ajax, The Dutch, The War: Football in Europe During the Second World War*, London, Orion, 2003

Kuper, Simon, *Football Against the Enemy*, London, Orion, 1994

McEnroe, John, *Serious: The Autobiography*, London, Little Brown, 2002

McGrath, Paul, *Back From the Brink: The Autobiography*, London, Century, 2006

Matthews, Sir Stanley: *The Way It Was: My Autobiography*, London, Headline, 2000

Maradona, Diego, *El Diego: The Autobiography of the World's Greatest Footballer*, London, Yellow Jersey, 2004

Minden, Eliza Gaynor, *Ballet Companion: A Dancer's Guide to the Technique, Traditions and Joys of Ballet*, London, Simon & Schuster, 2006

Mosley, James, *Ronaldo: The Journey of a Genius*, Edinburgh, Mainstream, 2005

Pearce, Stuart, *Psycho: The Autobiography*, London, Headline, 2000

Pelé, *Pelé: The Autobiography*, London, Simon & Schuster, 2006

Porter, Professor Roy, *Madness: A Brief History*, Oxford, OUP, 2002

Sacks, Oliver, *The Man Who Mistook His Wife for a Hat*, London, Picador, 1986

Tuan, Yi-Fu, *Escapism*, Baltimore, Johns Hopkins University Press, 1998

Vialli, Gianluca, and Marcotti, Gabriele, *The Italian Job: A Journey to the Heart of Two Great Footballing Cultures*, London, Bantam, 2006

Vieira, Patrick, *Vieira: My Autobiography*, London, Orion, 2005

Williams, Richard, *The Perfect 10: Football's Dreamers, Schemers, Playmakers and Playboys*, London, Faber & Faber, 2006

Wilson, Bob, *Behind the Network: My Autobiography*, London, Hodder & Stoughton , 2003

Wilson, Jonathan, *Behind the Curtain: Travels in Eastern European Football*, London, Orion, 2006

Winner, David, *Brilliant Orange: The Neurotic Genius of Dutch Football*, London, Bloomsbury, 2000

Wright, Ian, *Mr. Wright: The Explosive Autobiography of Ian Wright*, London, HarperCollins, 1996